Public Investment Planning in Civilian Nuclear Power

Public Investment Planning in Civilian Nuclear Power

John M. Vernon

Duke University Press
Durham, N.C. 1971

© 1971, Duke University Press
LCC card no. 78-132029
ISBN 0-8223-0237-3
Printed in the United States of
America by Kingsport Press, Inc.

To the memory of my father

Preface

This book represents a modest revision of my doctoral dissertation, which was completed at the Massachusetts Institute of Technology in 1966. The changes that have taken place in civilian nuclear power in the past three years have not been taken into account, although a number of footnotes have been added to call attention to changes where new data significantly differ from those used in the analysis.

The justification for investment by the United States Atomic Energy Commission in the development of advanced nuclear reactors for the production of electric power has centered upon conserving uranium. This study makes an economic evaluation of one specific development program, the advanced converter program.

Chapter 1 poses the basic problem: the development of advanced converter reactors in order to conserve physical units of uranium will only, by chance, coincide with an optimal intertemporal allocation of resources. Hence the aim of the study is to measure the impact on resource allocation.

Chapters 2 through 5 are concerned with the cost of producing electricity in light water nuclear plants. Light water plants are the first-generation nuclear plants that are *now* competitive with conventional fossil fuel power plants. These costs are important for our study because the benefits of the investment are taken to be the cost saving that advanced converter plants will have over light water plants. There are also some analytical problems in determining the cost of nuclear electric power that make a cost analysis interesting for its own sake. The cost chapters are quite detailed, however, and the reader who is primarily interested in benefit-cost analysis can profitably omit these four chapters.

The economics of the uranium industry is the subject of Chapter 6. Uranium prices are predicted for two cases: a nuclear power growth pattern with and without advanced converter reactors.

Chapter 7 uses the costs for light water plants and cost predictions for advanced converter plants to calculate the benefits of the development program. Because of the importance of uncertainty, a decision-tree approach to the evaluation of benefits is taken. A subjective probability distribution is developed for eighty-one possible outcomes of benefits. It is concluded that

vii

the program is, at best, a marginal social investment and that two of the three types of advanced converter reactors in the program should be abandoned.

I should like to thank Professors Sidney Alexander and Manson Benedict of the Massachusetts Institute of Technology, Mr. Abe Gerber and Dr. Paul Dragoumis of the American Electric Power Company, Mr. Tatsuo Suzuki of the Japan Development Bank, and Professor Peter B. Clark of Duke University for many helpful comments. Also, I should like to thank Drs. Sam Schurr and O. C. Herfindahl of Resources for the Future for their assistance in enabling me to spend the summer of 1968 reviewing the economics of nuclear power. My greatest debt is to Professor M. A. Adelman, my dissertation supervisor and good friend. Special thanks are due my mother for her encouragement and assistance. And, finally, I could have never completed this book without the understanding, inspiration, and able typing of my wife Jerry. The research and publication were financed by grants from Resources for the Future and the Duke University Research Council, respectively.

John M. Vernon

Durham, North Carolina
February 1969

Table of Contents

List of Illustrations

Tables

Figures

Public Investment Planning in Civilian Nuclear Power

Chapter 1. Introduction

> MR. O'BRIEN. You have to then weigh . . . against . . . how
> much should you spend, how much benefit is to be derived
> from the expenditure.
>
> REPRESENTATIVE HOSMER. Yes, and if you want to carry
> that one step further, you would tell the Atomic Energy
> Commission, [as I have] suggested from time to time, that
> they attempt to adapt some of the cost effectiveness prin-
> ciples in vogue at the Defense Department to their own
> operations and their own decisions relative to where they are
> going to put their money. It might not be a bad idea.
>
> Hearings before the Joint Committee on Atomic Energy, Congress
> of the United States, on *Private Ownership of Special Nuclear
> Materials, 1964,* June 1964, pp. 281–282.

In 1962, the United States Atomic Energy Commission submitted a now
well-known report to the President.[1] The President had instructed the commission to take a "new and hard look at the objectives, scope, and content
of a nuclear power development program in the light of the nation's prospective energy needs and resources."

The AEC stated in the report that "the development and exploitation of
nuclear electric power is clearly in the near- and long-term national interest."
It proposed a development plan consisting of three overlapping phases.[2]
In essence, the first phase was to develop the technically simplest kind of
nuclear reactor, viz., those of low fuel use efficiency. The second phase was
to develop reactors of an intermediate level of fuel use efficiency, and the
third phase was to develop the technically most difficult: reactors which
produce more fuel than they consume. In more specific terminology, the first-
generation reactors are light water, enriched uranium reactors, the second-

1. U.S. Atomic Energy Commission, *Civilian Nuclear Power: A Report to the President,
1962* (Oak Ridge, Tenn.: AEC Division of Technical Information, 1962).
2. The AEC reviewed and reaffirmed the development plan in 1967. See U.S. Atomic
Energy Commission, *Civilian Nuclear Power: The 1967 Supplement to the 1962 Report to the
President,* February 1967.

generation ones are advanced converter or advanced thermal reactors, and the third-generation reactors are breeders.[3]

That AEC participation in the development of light water reactors should be drawing to a close was first made known in December 1963. The Jersey Central Power and Light Company announced that it had accepted a proposal of the General Electric Company to construct a 515-megawatt nuclear electric plant, and that it would seek "no government financial assistance . . . in connection with the construction or operation of the station."[4] Although no nuclear plants were sold in 1964, in 1965 and early 1966 plans for 9,219 megawatts of light water nuclear capacity were announced by electric power companies.[5] There is general agreement that the first phase of the AEC development program is nearing termination. For example, AEC Commissioner Ramey, in an October 1965 speech, said that the development of light water reactors "has reached a stage which permits the Commission to reduce its R and D support, and to turn toward more advanced systems."[6]

The Problem

The AEC described the second phase of the development program in hearings before the Joint Committee on Atomic Energy in March and April 1965.[7] Technical knowledge gained in earlier stages of research made it

3. Predicted fuel use efficiency factors for the three broad reactor types are: light water — 1 percent, advanced converters (high-temperature, gas-cooled) — 4 percent, breeders — 80 percent. Fuel use efficiency factor is defined as the percentage of the atoms of fertile plus fissile material mined (to sustain the reactor) which fission. One type of advanced converter, the seed and blanket, is predicted to have a fuel use efficiency factor of 50 percent. It is, however, optimized for self-sustaining breeding rather than lowest cost. The predicted power cost for the seed and blanket is slightly higher than the cost predicted for the high-temperature, gas-cooled reactor. Predictions are given in U.S. Congress, Joint Committee on Atomic Energy, *AEC Authorizing Legislation, Fiscal Year 1966, Part 3*, 89th Congress, 1st Session, March and April 1965, pp. 1758, 1767.

4. Jersey Central Power and Light Company, *Report on Economic Analysis for Oyster Creek Nuclear Electric Generating Station*, 17 February 1964, p. 1.

5. The reader may be interested to learn the record of announcements of light water nuclear capacity through September 1969. To place these figures in perspective, nuclear megawatts percentages of total nuclear and fossil megawatts are shown in parentheses: 1965, 6,009 (27); 1966, 22,477 (53); 1967, 26,460 (45); 1968, 14,803 (38); 1969 (through September), 4,029 (13). Nuclear plant orders peaked in 1967 and have declined sharply since that year. Serious construction delays with higher costs and public concern with radiation and thermal effects of nuclear plants have combined to make nuclear plants less attractive vis-à-vis fossil plants (U.S. Atomic Energy Commission, *The Nuclear Industry 1969*, December 1969, p. 134).

6. James T. Ramey, "A Review of Nuclear Programs of Interest to the Oil and Gas Industry," speech at the Texas Mid-Continent Oil and Gas Association, Fort Worth, Tex. 19 October 1965, p. 9.

7. *AEC Authorizing Legislation, Fiscal Year 1966, Part 3*.

4

possible for the AEC to select three types of reactors for the advanced converter program. One of the three is at the stage of development permitting a large-scale prototype to be constructed. The others are less advanced.[8] Chairman Seaborg and Commissioner Ramey of the AEC have estimated that the cost to the government for the total advanced converter development program would be $300 million.[9]

Concurrently, the AEC is supporting research and development in the third phase of the program. The expenditure on development of fast breeder reactors in fiscal year 1964 was approximately $16 million, and estimates for fiscal years 1965 and 1966 are approximately $21 million and $24 million, respectively.[10] Chairman Seaborg has been quoted as anticipating a government funding level of about $40 million for fast breeder development in fiscal year 1967.[11]

Chairman Seaborg testified to the Joint Committee on Atomic Energy that "sometime in the 1980s we would expect to have large, economic, high-gain breeder reactors."[12] When asked what the effect of technical knowledge gained in the advanced converter program would be upon breeder development, he replied that "it would change the date [of achieving breeders], but certainly by no more than a year."[13] Since there is no technical necessity for the second phase of the program to precede the third phase, the decision to develop advanced converter reactors should be based on the economics of these reactors alone. It is our contention that an *economic* analysis of the need for advanced converter reactors has not been made and is badly needed.

The justification for the second phase of the development program is made questionable by other countries' policies in nuclear power development. Belgian nuclear policy, for example, "tends to favor continuing with pressurized water reactors until breeders become commercially feasible."[14] The Karlsruhe nuclear center, the nuclear industry association, and the Federal Science Ministry have urged that West Germany's breeder development be accelerated. The objective of the accelerated program would be to complete a 1,000-megawatt breeder considerably earlier than the present 1980 target.[15] West Germany's "move is in line with a general quickening of

8. Congress authorized $132.4 million in fiscal year 1966 budget for the construction of large prototypes of two advanced reactors: the high-temperature, gas-cooled and the seed and blanket (*Nucleonics*, 23 [June 1965]: 21). Technical problems have since induced the AEC to postpone the seed and blanket prototype indefinitely (*Nucleonics*, 24 [February 1966]: 17).
9. *AEC Authorizing Legislation, Fiscal Year 1966, Part 3*, p. 1386.
10. Ibid., p. 1718.
11. *Nucleonics*, 23 (November 1965): 23.
12. *AEC Authorizing Legislation, Fiscal Year 1966, Part 3*, p. 1385.
13. Ibid., p. 1387.
14. *Nucleonics*, 23 (December 1965): 26.
15. *Nucleonics*, 23 (November 1965): 26.

fast-breeder activity in Europe: Sweden is considering an amplified program, Spain is doing likewise, and Britain is increasingly optimistic."[16]

Investment in advanced converter prototypes, from the AEC viewpoint, is an interim conservation measure to bring about in the 1970s and 1980s the installation of nuclear plants which will consume fuel more efficiently than the light water reactor plants. The pressure on nuclear fuel resources is expected to be greatly reduced in the 1980s by the introduction of breeder reactors. Breeders will extract some eighty times more energy from a unit of uranium than can light water reactors. This objective appears to be generally subscribed to by both the AEC and the Joint Committee on Atomic Energy. For example, the director of the Division of Naval Reactors testified that "one of the main objectives of the Commission is to try to make our uranium and thorium resources last longer."[17]

The report, "Analysis of Advanced Converters and Self-Sustaining Breeders," was the primary document presented by the AEC to the Joint Committee on Atomic Energy in support of the advanced converter program.[18] The concluding paragraph of that report illustrates the AEC concern with conservation. It should be pointed out that although "substantial direct economic benefits" are suggested, no attempt was made to estimate these benefits.

> The development and commercial application of advanced thermal reactors can fulfill important objectives of the overall civilian nuclear power program. The . . . case studies indicate that if the future nuclear complex includes these reactors, natural uranium requirements are reduced. Any such reduction would serve to stretch out the availability of the lower cost uranium resources. Besides effecting changes in the trends in requirements for natural uranium, the advanced thermal reactors offer substantial direct economic benefits resulting from their more effective use of our nuclear fuel resources.[19]

The AEC analysis examined a number of different growth patterns of nuclear power capacity and calculated the cumulative uranium requirements for each. It clearly demonstrated that cumulative uranium requirements would be lower with advanced converter reactors than if they were absent. The calculation of uranium requirements under a number of growth patterns is not the object of our criticism. This exercise is important in predicting the price of uranium. We criticize the report for stopping at that point. The expectation that the consumption of physical units of uranium

16. Ibid.
17. *AEC Authorizing Legislation, Fiscal Year 1966, Part 3*, p. 1411.
18. Ibid., pp. 1751–1768.
19. Ibid., p. 1764.

will be lower with the advanced converter program than they will be without the program is an insufficient basis for an economic decision. The relevant further calculation should have been to determine the saving to the economy resulting from the lower uranium requirement. The notion that there is a "trade off" between the cost of the program and the saving which it creates was not considered.[20]

Figure 1–1 should provide a clear explanation of the problem. We shall abstract from time, although greater electricity output can be associated with later periods of time. The chart portrays a smoothly substitutable production function for the output of electricity. Only two inputs are shown, uranium and development capital. Capital equipment and labor are also certainly needed for electricity generation, but they are assumed to be inde-

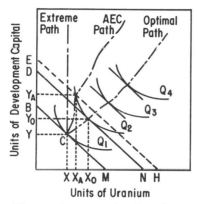

Figure 1–1. Production function for nuclear power development

20. This is not strictly correct. In the Joint Committee on Atomic Energy Hearings in March 1965 (p. 1386) one exchange between Representative Hosmer and Chairman Seaborg had to do with comparing benefits with cost. Unfortunately, the benefits were unrelated to the cost. After Commissioner Ramey had estimated that the total cost of the advanced converter program would be $300 million, this discussion followed:

> REPRESENTATIVE HOSMER. Against that figure, I think someone has estimated that the developmental work which has been done in the nuclear energy field under sponsorship of the Government is now resulting in at least a billion dollars a year saving to American citizens in the form of power rates that have not been increased because we have this form of power.
> Is that somewhere in the ball park?
> DR. SEABORG. Yes, that is in the ball park. That is an estimate that has been made and I think on a good basis.
> REPRESENTATIVE HOSMER. So we are not just pursuing science for science's sake, we are paying dividends to the taxpayers then.
> DR. SEABORG. Yes, I think so.

pendent of the amounts of uranium and development capital and are irrelevant for our purposes. A "unit" of development capital is defined as the amount of development services forthcoming from an expenditure of an arbitrary sum of money. Development services are those which increase the efficiency of uranium utilization. The level of electricity output is represented by a Q contour or isoquant ($Q_1 < Q_2 < Q_3 \ldots$).

The slopes of the PP lines are the ratios of the prices of the two inputs. Therefore, at points where PP is tangent to an isoquant, an optimal allocation of resources is achieved. The ratio of the price of uranium to its marginal physical product is equal to the ratio of the price of development capital to its marginal physical product. For any particular total cost (total cost is measured in units of uranium at the horizontal axis intersection with PP), the isoquant to which PP is tangent is the maximum output. Conversely, for the output of a given isoquant, the PP line tangent to the isoquant defines the minimum cost. The line labeled "optimal path" is the locus of all such tangencies and therefore gives the optimal development expenditures for the given price ratio.

The line labeled "AEC path" is an example of a path likely to be followed in the pursuit of the goal of conservation of nuclear fuel resources (conservation here having the simple meaning of reducing current resource use). As will be noted, this notion of conservation has no operational meaning in the sense of defining a particular development plan. At the limit, it would mean using an infinite number of units of development capital in order to consume zero additional units of uranium. This case is illustrated by the vertical line labeled "extreme path." We will assume that the AEC path lies between the extreme path and the optimal path. It could, of course, coincide with the optimal path, but a priori this is unlikely since it would happen only by chance.

We will assume that the United States is currently at point C in figure 1-1. In order to meet the expected larger output requirement, Q_2, a decision must be made as to the amount of additional input required. To achieve an optimal allocation of resources, assuming no price change, it is necessary to increase the input of uranium by OX_0-OX and to increase the input of development capital by OY_0-OY. The cost required for this expansion is equal to ON-OM units of uranium. If this increase in output were to be met by moving out the AEC path, fewer units of uranium (thereby conserving uranium) and more units of development capital would be required than by following the optimal path. The point is that for an expansion on the AEC path the cost (OH-OM units of uranium) is greater than for an expansion on the optimal path (ON-OM units of uranium). The excess cost can be measured as OH-ON units of uranium or as OE-OD units of development capital.

8

One major assumption made in this simple analysis is that the price ratio will remain constant, but this is probably not realistic. It can be argued that if the optimal path is followed the price of uranium relative to the price of development capital will increase. The greater demand for uranium along the optimal path than along the AEC path may cause the relative price of uranium to rise. Therefore, the optimal path with changing price would probably lie somewhere between the AEC path and the optimal path of figure 1–1, as illustrated in figure 1–2.

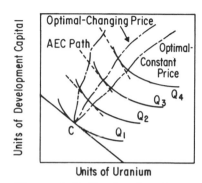

Figure 1–2. Production function with changing price ratio of inputs

The depiction of the problem by the two diagrams is clearly an over-simplification. It assumes that some direct and continuous relation between units of development capital and increased fuel use efficiency exists. In actuality, only one point of this function is thought to be known, and there is great uncertainty about even that.[21] Another strong assumption is that capital equipment is unaffected by the amount of development capital applied, which is not realistic because development services must be embodied in capital equipment. Furthermore, it is assumed that the higher-efficiency technology created by a unit of development capital is immediately incorporated into all new nuclear plants.

Despite the numerous and restrictive assumptions made, the essential character of the problem is not seriously distorted. The goals set by the AEC for the advanced converter program are such that most of the support and justification for the program are concerned with conserving physical units of nuclear fuel resources. It would therefore be mere coincidence if the program also achieved an optimal allocation of resources.

---

21. The point is determined by the cost of the advanced converter program and the fuel efficiency of those reactors.

The purpose of this study is to make an *economic* analysis of the advanced converter program. The analysis will use as its criterion of success an optimal intertemporal allocation of resources, although there are certainly other criteria which could be selected. Leadership in advanced converter technology could conceivably be an effective instrument of foreign policy. The goal might be full employment, and the investment would serve to boost aggregate demand. The AEC has apparently seized upon the goal of conservation of nuclear fuel resources. A properly conceived conservation policy could, of course, be consistent with the optimal intertemporal allocation of resources, but our examination of the AEC's concept of conservation does not lead to this conclusion. It is for this reason that this analysis is made.

The Plan of the Study

To consider the economics of government investment in nuclear power development without considering the role of government in other areas of energy supply is wrong. "It is a bit anomalous to calculate that nuclear energy is economic because conventional fuel costs are high in certain areas when it is merely another arm of the government which is keeping them high."[22] An economically correct approach requires the simultaneous examination of government policy in all areas.

Nevertheless, recognizing explicitly the lack of a general programming approach as a limitation, a partial analysis of the AEC advanced converter development program can be enlightening. Our concern will not be with the total AEC program in relation to other energy sectors but will be with whether the program as it stands would be better with or without the second phase.[23] It is assumed here that there is no significant technical reason for the second phase of the program to precede the third phase. Furthermore, it is assumed that the present time schedule of breeder development is accurate (although we will vary the date of breeder introduction). If breeders are not economic until a much later date, the case for advanced converter reactors is made stronger.

A more general approach could be followed within the nuclear energy sector alone. Rather than taking the date of introduction of breeders as a parameter, the amount and timing of investment in breeder development could also be viewed as variables. The uncertainties would be greater, and the benefit calculation made more difficult both in measurement and concept.

22. M. A. Adelman, "Efficiency of Resource Use in Crude Petroleum," *Southern Economic Journal,* 31 (October 1964): 112.
23. Account is implicitly taken of other energy sectors by projections of the rate of growth of nuclear capacity.

To confine this study within the technical competence of the analyst, and to manageable proportions, only a benefit-cost analysis of the advanced converter program will be made. The benefit is defined as the reduction in the cost of electric power generation to the economy in the future which can be attributed to the advanced converter reactors. Cost is the investment in the development of these reactors. Chapter 7 will deal more thoroughly with the application and theory of benefit-cost analysis, and will also examine the economic basis for the government role in the development of nuclear power.

Several benefit-cost analyses of the total nuclear power program have been made in the past.[24] They are not directly relevant to our study because each was concerned with the benefits and costs of the total AEC power program, not with a particular segment of that program.[25] The AEC made a benefit analysis in the appendixes to its 1962 report to the President. Its figure for cumulative savings with zero discount rate through the year 2000 was $30 billion. The associated cost was not reported. To our knowledge, a benefit-cost analysis of the advanced converter program has not been made.

The measurement of the benefit of the program is particularly difficult because of a number of uncertainties: future nuclear power costs, the success of the development program, technological change in alternative electricity production methods, and the demand for electricity in the future. For this and other reasons, the benefit-cost analysis has been criticized in evaluating the AEC program. The following quotation is taken from a speech made by an AEC commissioner in February 1965.

> As can be readily appreciated [a benefit-cost analysis] is very difficult, if not impossible, to apply to R and D work due to the basic problem of forcasting the costs and the benefits of a proposed project.
> In the Energy Study, the use of cost-benefit techniques, coupled with the selection of a high discount rate, could have the effect, if not the intent, of hamstringing atomic power.[26]

24. Edward F. Renshaw, "Atomic Power: Research Costs and Social Returns," *Land Economics,* 35 (August 1959): 222; Keith L. Harms, *Economic Considerations Bearing on Civilian Nuclear Power Development,* Supplement II to the Report of the Ad Hoc Committee on Atomic Policy of the Atomic Industrial Forum, March 1962; J. A. Hasson, *The Economics of Nuclear Power* (London: Longmans, Green, 1965), p. 70.

25. However, two relevant studies were published in 1969: Paul W. MacAvoy, *Economic Strategy for Developing Nuclear Breeder Reactors* (Cambridge, Mass.: MIT Press, 1969), and U.S. Atomic Energy Commission, *Cost-Benefit Analysis of the U.S. Breeder Reactor Program,* Report WASH-1126, 1969.

26. James T. Ramey, "The Role of Planning in the Atomic Energy Program," speech at Lynchburg, Va., 16 February 1965, p. 17. The energy study referred to by the commissioner included an illustrative benefit-cost analysis of the total AEC civilian power program. Its purpose was to demonstrate the use of such a technique in evaluating any energy research and development investment, and was not intended to be a complete analysis. See U.S. Interdepartmental Energy Study, *Energy R & D and National Progress* (Washington: Government Printing Office, 1965).

It is certainly true that benefit-cost analysis is very difficult to apply to research and development work.[27] But an investment decision has been made based upon *some* expectation of the future, and it is only foolishness to avoid making explicit one's predictions of the future. Furthermore, the *purpose* of benefit-cost analysis is to evaluate whether or not atomic power *should* be hamstrung.

A large part of the study must be devoted to the cost of power produced in light water reactor plants. Knowledge of the cost is important for two reasons. First, the benefit to the economy is taken as the difference in cost of light water and advanced converter reactors. Second, the AEC intends to develop advanced converter reactors only to a level of economic attractiveness to private power companies. The actual installation of advanced converter reactors will depend upon the private investment decisions of these firms. These decisions, in turn, will depend upon the comparative costs of alternative methods of producing electricity. In general, at locations where nuclear power is considered to have the advantage over fossil fuel and hydroelectric power, a further choice will be made between light water and advanced converter power. Unless advanced converter plants promise costs sufficiently lower than light water plants (enough to offset the greater experience and certainty associated with light water reactors), firms will choose to install only the proven nuclear plants.

The cost of producing electricity is usually divided into two main categories, capital cost and fuel cost, and we will observe the conventional dichotomy. One small exception is made: the working capital requirement is an integral part of the nuclear fuel cycle and will be considered as a fuel cost.[28]

Chapter 2 will discuss the cost of nuclear power and its relation to the theory of production. It will be shown that the theory of production can be easily adapted to nuclear power and is helpful in understanding the more important economic relationships. Because of the many technical factors affecting cost, the first part of the chapter will be a brief description of the technology.

Chapter 3 will be devoted to the capital cost. Chapters 4 and 5 will study the interrelations between the key variables affecting the fuel cost. The economics of fuel enrichment, fabrication, and reprocessing will be ex-

27. The application of benefit-cost techniques to the advanced converter program should be simpler than to the breeder program. The advanced converters are in the development stage of building large-scale prototypes. Unforeseen secondary benefits are less likely to occur than in the breeder program, which is in an earlier development, or even research, stage.

28. Two other relatively small costs will not be studied: operation and maintenance costs and nuclear insurance costs. We shall assume that these two costs will be the same for either type plant, thereby canceling in the benefit-cost analysis.

amined, and chapter 5 will also investigate the factors affecting the future plutonium credit. Chapter 6 will analyze the determination of uranium price.

The cost of advanced converter nuclear power is no less important to our analysis than the cost of light water nuclear power. However, much more is known about the latter. The first light water nuclear plant was placed in service in a utility grid in 1957. In contrast, large prototypes of the advanced converter reactors will not be completed until the early 1970s. The best available cost estimates for the advanced converter reactors are contained in a study published by the Oak Ridge National Laboratory (ORNL) in January 1965.[29] This study will be especially useful for our analysis because it compares costs of advanced converter reactors and light water reactors on a standardized basis. This is appropriate because the benefit-cost analysis is concerned with relative costs and not absolute ones.

Chapter 7, the benefit-cost analysis, will summarize and project the costs of light water and advanced converter nuclear power over the horizon of the study. For this purpose, only the cost of one type of advanced reactor will be selected, viz., the high-temperature, gas-cooled reactor. There are several reasons for this decision. Of the three types of advanced reactors in the current program, only the high-temperature, gas-cooled reactor (HTGR) is included in the January 1965 ORNL study. The bulk of the study was prepared in 1964 when slightly different designs of the other reactors were thought to be most promising. The HTGR was estimated, in the March 1965 congressional hearings, to have costs midway between the costs of the other two advanced reactors; it should therefore serve as a representative advanced reactor. Furthermore, it will apparently be the first reactor to reach the large prototype stage.

The results of the benefit-cost analysis will also be presented in chapter 7. Results will be reported for various values of key parameters, and qualifications and implications for policy will be discussed.

29. M. W. Rosenthal et al., *A Comparative Evaluation of Advanced Converters,* AEC Research and Development Report, ORNL-3686, January 1965. Referred to hereafter as the Rosenthal report.

Chapter 2. Nuclear Power Technology and Cost

Any attempt to understand the analytical framework of the cost of nuclear power must be preceded by some knowledge of nuclear technology. A number of excellent books discuss the technology in detail,[1] but it should be helpful to outline the major points here. Following the summary of technology, the cost of nuclear power will be considered in the context of the economic theory of production.

Technology

The diagram in figure 2–1 shows the essential components of a nuclear power plant. The nuclear reactor merely replaces the fossil fuel boiler of conventional plants.

The nuclear fission reaction takes place within the core. Since it is this reaction which provides the energy for power production, it will be worthwhile to examine the principle of fission.

The Einstein equation,

$$E = MC^2, \tag{2–1}$$

where E is energy in ergs, M is mass in grams, and C is the velocity of light $(2.998 \times 10^{10}$ centimeters per second), shows the equivalence of mass and energy. In a fission reaction, an atom of fissile material is bombarded with a subatomic particle, a neutron. The neutron causes the nucleus of the atom to split into two fragments and to release two or three more neutrons. The important point is that the actual mass of the atomic particles after fission is less than the mass before fission. The difference, or mass defect, is converted into energy. The exact amount can be calculated from the Einstein equation. As an illustration, one pound of fissile material should be capable of producing the same amount of energy as 1,400 tons of coal.[2]

A nuclear chain reaction is made possible by the fact that two or three

1. For example, Donald J. Hughes, *On Nuclear Energy* (Cambridge, Mass.: Harvard University Press, 1957), and Samuel Glasstone and Alexander Sesonske, *Nuclear Reactor Engineering* (Princeton: Van Nostrand, 1963).
2. Glasstone and Sesonske, p. 15.

additional neutrons are produced in the fission process. An average of 2.43 neutrons is emitted for every uranium-235 nucleus fissioned. For a self-sustaining reaction, only one neutron is required for further fissioning. Consequently, the additional neutrons provide a margin. Some of the excess neutrons may be captured by control rod material or structural parts of the

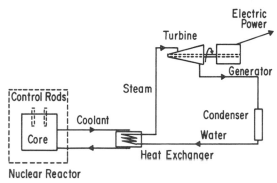

Figure 2–1. Nuclear power plant diagram

reactor. The major problem in increasing the fuel use efficiency of reactors is to divert more neutrons from wasteful losses and into fissile material production.[3]

There is only one naturally occurring, readily fissionable material. This is uranium-235, which is present in the amount of 0.7 percent in natural uranium, the balance being almost entirely uranium-238. Two other fissionable (or fissile) materials are uranium-233 and plutonium-239. Such materials as uranium-238 or thorium-232 are fertile materials; that is, they can be converted into fissile isotopes (plutonium-239 and uranium-233, respectively) upon capture of a neutron.

Two basic types of reactors are the fast reactors and the thermal, or slow, reactors. Fission neutrons have kinetic energy much greater than atoms of the reactor core. A property of uranium-238 is that it absorbs these "fast" neutrons to such an extent that few are left to fission uranium-235. However, by "slowing" down the neutrons, the absorptive capability of uranium-238 is greatly reduced.[4] The neutrons are slowed down by collision with atoms of low mass which have the ability to reduce neutron speed without themselves

3. As was pointed out in chapter 1, fuel use efficiency is the percentage of fertile plus fissile material mined (to sustain the reactor) which undergoes fission. The importance of extracting a greater amount of energy from the same amount of fuel (increasing fuel use efficiency) is obvious. Creating "by-product" fissile material which can be fissioned in a subsequent fuel loading, if not concurrently, is the key to increasing fuel use.

4. Fast reactors must have more highly enriched fuel than thermal reactors. That is to say, the ratio of uranium-238 to uranium-235 is smaller in fast reactors than in thermal ones.

absorbing many neutrons. The material used to reduce the kinetic energy of neutrons to a slow, or thermal, equilibrium is known as the moderator. Thus reactors without moderators are fast reactors, and those with moderators are thermal reactors.

To increase fuel use efficiency, it is important to increase the average number of neutrons captured by fertile material per neutron furthering the chain reaction. The average number of neutrons emitted per neutron absorbed in fuel is therefore crucial. Table 2–1 gives these nuclear properties for fissile materials in both fast and thermal reactors.

Table 2–1. Average number of neutrons emitted per neutron absorbed in fuel

	U-233	U-235	PU-239	Natural U
Thermal neutrons	2.27	2.06	2.10	1.33
Fast neutrons	2.60	2.18	2.74	1.09

Source: Samuel Glasstone and Alexander Sesonske, *Nuclear Reactor Engineering* (Princeton: Van Nostrand, 1963), p. 154.

Since one neutron is required to maintain the chain reaction, one less than each of the numbers in the table is available for converting fertile material into fissile material. There are always losses of neutrons by leakage and parasitic capture in other parts of the reactor. Hence, to achieve breeding (in which at least one neutron is absorbed in fertile material per neutron absorbed in fissile material), table 2–1 shows that the nuclear properties of plutonium in fast reactors and uranium-233 in both thermal and fast reactors are the most favorable.

In the current state of technology, thermal reactors are well understood, while fast reactors are in an earlier stage of development. Fast reactors require highly enriched fuel and must operate at high power density. Technical difficulties are associated with the fuel handling requirements of fast reactors because of the compact reactor design, the sodium environment, and the severe fission-product-decay cooling problems after high-density operation.[5] These are some of the reasons why breeder reactors are not predicted to be ready for commercial use until the 1980s. The figures in table 2–1 nevertheless make clear the advantage of fast reactors.

The reactor coolant is the liquid or gas which transfers energy in the form of heat from the core to the heat exchanger, or steam turbine. The ideal coolant should combine good heat transfer properties with the nuclear properties of a good moderator, i.e., low neutron absorption.

5. L. J. Koch, "The Future of Fast Breeders," *Nucleonics,* 21 (June 1963): 73.

Another basic component of a nuclear reactor is the control rod system. Control rods are made of neutron-absorbing material and are inserted into the core to slow the reaction and withdrawn to speed the reaction.

Many possible arrangements of fissile and fertile fuel, moderator, and coolant can constitute a nuclear reactor system. Six types have emerged as principal contenders for full-scale electric power production. These six are (a) pressurized water, (b) boiling water, (c) gas cooled, (d) heavy water moderated, organic cooled, (e) heavy water cooled, and (f) sodium cooled.[6]

The first two reactors on the list are generally referred to in this study as light water reactors. These are the predominant reactors in use on United States power grids. The third and fourth reactors are advanced converters. A third advanced reactor, the seed and blanket, is not listed; it can be considered as a variant of the pressurized water reactor. The most extensive use of the heavy water cooled reactor has been made in Canada. Natural uranium is the preferred fuel in Canada, and as table 2–1 demonstrates, neutron conservation is essential with this fuel. Heavy water, though more costly, has lower neutron absorptive capacity than light water and is therefore an appropriate coolant for natural uranium reactors.[7] The last type of reactor on the list is a promising one for fast breeding.

To show the essential difference between light water and advanced converter reactors, table 2–2 is reproduced from the March 1965 congressional hearings.

In our benefit-cost analysis we will compare light water power costs with the costs of a representative advanced converter reactor, the high-temperature, gas-cooled reactor. Thus it is well to point out the significant advantage in thermal efficiency of this advanced reactor over the light water one. Thermal efficiency is the percentage of energy released in the core which is ultimately transformed into electrical energy. This efficiency is roughly proportional to the temperature of steam entering the turbine. Table 2–2 shows the coolant outlet temperature of the high-temperature, gas-cooled reactor to be about 800° F. higher than that of the light water reactor.

Another important technical difference between the reactors can be seen from a comparison of the natural uranium requirements of each in table 2–3. As we have discussed before, improvement in fuel use efficiency is

6. R. K. Evans, "Nuclear Power Reactors," *Power,* March 1965, p. S-7.

7. The reason that Canada prefers natural uranium as fuel is important. In the United States, during World War II, an investment of over $2 billion was made in gaseous diffusion plants for military purposes. These plants can increase the concentration of the fissile isotope, uranium-235, in natural uranium. This improves the chain reaction capability of uranium and reduces the degree of neutron conservation effort required. A large diffusion plant investment must be viewed as a substitute for the added cost of neutron conservation measures. Canada has chosen the latter alternative.

Table 2-2. General plant characteristics

	Light water		Advanced converter reactors		
	PWR	BWR	HWOCR	HTGR	SBR
Coolant	H_2O	H_2O	Organic	Helium	H_2O
Moderator	H_2O	H_2O	D_2O	Graphite	H_2O
Net electric power, mw	1,002	1,000	1,000	1,008	1,000
Thermal power, mw	3,220	3,194	3,030	2,270	3,200
Net thermal efficiency, percentage	31	31	33	44	31
Coolant temperature °F					
Inlet	546	291	536	720	520
Outlet	598	546	760	1,470	582
Coolant pressure psia	2,050	1,015	350	450	2,000
Coolant flow, 10^6 lbs/hr	160	114	90	8.3	138

Note: PWR = pressurized water reactor; BWR = boiling water reactor; HWOCR = heavy-water, organic-cooled reactor; HTGR = high-temperature, gas-cooled reactor; SBR = seed and blanket reactor.

Source: U.S. Congress, Joint Committee on Atomic Energy, *AEC Authorizing Legislation Fiscal Year 1966, Part 3*, 89th Congress, 1st Session, March and April 1965, p. 1400.

brought about by increasing the average number of neutrons captured in fertile material (thereby producing additional fissile material) per neutron furthering the chain reaction. Advanced converter reactors have higher fuel use efficiencies than light water reactors because their designs give more emphasis to increasing the average number of neutrons available for capture in fertile material, and subsequently, to "burning" the fissile material created. Of course, the designer should bear in mind the "trade-off" between increasing the fuel use efficiency and increasing the capital cost of the reactor (the increment in capital cost must not be greater than the saving from higher fuel use efficiency).

A more detailed technical description of the nuclear fuel cycle will be deferred until chapter 4, but it will be helpful to sketch the major steps in the cycle before proceeding with the second part of this chapter.

The fuel cycle for light water plants begins at the enrichment step. The Atomic Energy Commission operates three large gaseous diffusion plants which enrich natural uranium in the uranium-235 isotope. The enriched uranium must then be fabricated into fuel elements, which are transported to the reactor site and inserted into the core. After the fission reaction, or irradiation period, the spent fuel elements must be stored until the radiation level is sufficiently reduced for shipment. The elements are then shipped to a chemical processing plant, where the fissile material (plutonium) created

Table 2–3. Natural uranium requirements

	Inventory STU_3O_8/eMW [a]	Makeup STU_3O_8/eMW year [b]	
Light water			
High estimate	1.0	0.16	
Low estimate	0.7	0.13	
Heavy water organic			
Uranium	0.2	0.09	
Thorium	0.7	0.025	
High temperature gas			
High estimate	0.9	0.04	
Low estimate	0.6	0.025	
Seed blanket			
High estimate	1.0	0.09	for 5 full power years, zero thereafter
Low estimate	0.7	0.08	for 5 full power years, zero thereafter

[a] STU_3O_8/eMW = short tons U_3O_8 per installed electrical megawatt.
[b] STU_3O_8/eMW year = short tons U_3O_8 per full-power electrical megawatt year of output.
Source: AEC Authorizing Legislation Fiscal Year 1966, Part 3, p. 1401.

during irradiation is extracted. The depleted uranium is then returned to the gaseous diffusion plants for reenrichment, thereby completing the cycle. This cycle discussed above is not, of course, unalterable. For example, in the future it may be possible to use plutonium as a fuel in light water reactors. Hence, rather than returning plutonium to the AEC, it would be shipped to the fuel fabrication facility.

Theory

The theory of production provides a useful framework for our discussion of the cost of nuclear power. In its most elementary form, a single-valued continuous production function with continuous first- and second-order partial derivatives is postulated. Two variable inputs, X and Y, are used in producing the output, Q. Figure 2–2 portrays the production function for selected levels of output, Q_1, Q_2, and Q_3 (where $Q_1 < Q_2 < Q_3$).

The ratio of the prices of X and Y, P_x/P_y, is given by the slope of the line

PM. Minimum cost for output Q_2 is achieved by the allocation of inputs specified by the point of tangency between *PM* and the Q_2 isoquant.

$$Q = f(X,Y) \ldots \text{the production function} \qquad (2\text{-}2)$$

and

$$\text{cost} = P_x X + P_y Y. \qquad (2\text{-}3)$$

The problem is to minimize cost subject to the constraint of the production function (alternatively, we could maximize output subject to the cost function constraint). An equivalent problem is to minimize

$$V = P_x X + P_y Y + \gamma [Q - f(X,Y)] \qquad (2\text{-}4)$$

where γ is the Lagrange multiplier. Taking partial derivatives and setting them equal to zero gives

$$\partial V / \partial X = P_x - \gamma \partial f / \partial X = 0 \qquad (2\text{-}5)$$
$$\partial V / \partial Y = P_y - \gamma \partial f / \partial Y = 0. \qquad (2\text{-}6)$$

Dividing equation 2–5 by equation 2–6 gives the first order condition for cost minimization: the ratio of prices of X and Y equals the ratio of marginal products of X and Y.

$$P_x / P_y = \partial f / \partial X \Big/ \partial f / \partial Y \qquad (2\text{-}7)$$

Since the slope of Q_2 is $\partial f / \partial X \Big/ \partial f / \partial Y$, this proves that the tangency condition shown in figure 2–2 determines minimum cost. Rewriting equation 2–7 as

$$\partial f / \partial X / P_x = \partial f / \partial Y / P_y \qquad (2\text{-}8)$$

demonstrates that to minimize cost the firm will equate the marginal product attributable to the last dollar spent on input X to the marginal product attributable to the last dollar spent on input Y. This can easily be extended to any number of inputs, in which case the condition for minimum cost becomes

$$\partial f / \partial X / P_x = \partial f / \partial Y / P_y = \partial f / \partial Z / P_z = \ldots \qquad (2\text{-}9)$$

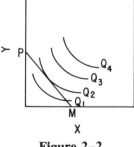

Figure 2–2

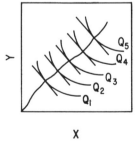

Figure 2–3

20

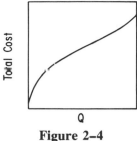

Figure 2–4

The locus of all possible tangencies between price ratios of inputs and isoquants defines the long-run cost function. This is shown in figure 2–3. In figure 2–4 the cost curve defined by the tangencies is plotted in its conventional form, and figure 2–5 carries the analysis a step further by showing the average and marginal cost functions.[8]

Our analysis has yet to relate the theory sketched above to the cost of nuclear power. We do so now. The long-run cost function of nuclear power is the subject of our inquiry. If we think of output, Q, as being kilowatt-hours of electricity and the two inputs, X and Y, as being capital and fuel, the basic conceptual framework for our analysis is complete. Of course our degree of abstraction is too great to be directly applicable to nuclear power cost. We must consider many inputs, not just two. Our knowledge of the cost of nuclear power over the range of all outputs is nil. All inputs are not smoothly substitutable for other inputs.

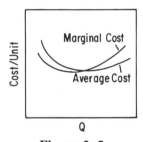

Figure 2–5

In our analysis of cost, the subject of chapters 3–6, we will concentrate on one particular plant size. Economies of scale are significant in nuclear power, as the chapter on capital cost will make clear. The largest plant for which good cost estimates are available is one of 1,000 megawatts (electrical).

8. For a complete exposition of the theory of production, the reader is referred to Thomas H. Naylor and John M. Vernon, *Microeconomics and Decision Models of the Firm* (New York: Harcourt, Brace and World, 1969).

Plants larger than this may well have lower cost, but the costs are too uncertain at this time. Since increasing returns are present throughout the range of plant sizes up to 1,000 megawatts, the best estimate of long-run marginal cost is the cost of power produced in a 1,000-megawatt plant.

Figure 2–6 should clarify the point discussed above. At the present time it is not known whether economies or diseconomies will prevail at output levels greater than those associated with a 1,000-megawatt plant. Assuming that long-run average cost is near its minimum at the output level of a 1,000-megawatt plant, long-run marginal cost should be approximately equal to long-run average cost. Also, short-run average cost of a 1,000-megawatt plant should be equal to long-run average cost at this assumed minimum and should therefore be a reasonable estimate of long-run marginal cost.

It should be stressed that a cost function is never found so easily as is implied by the theory described above, which assumes a known production function. In an industry such as nuclear energy in which technology is continually changing and better ways of doing the same thing are frequently discovered, the production function is difficult to pin down.

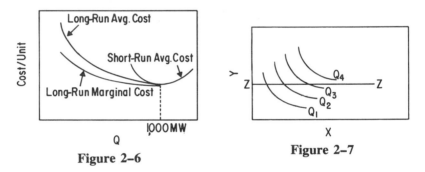

Figure 2–6

Figure 2–7

The decision to concentrate on the cost of power produced in a 1,000-megawatt plant makes it possible to consider the capital, or fixed, cost and the fuel, or variable, cost separately. In effect, this means that the plant is fixed and we can only vary inputs affecting the fuel cost. Thus, in our simple two-input theory in figure 2–7, with Y fixed, the cost function can only be generated by moving along line ZZ. Total cost is the sum of the cost of the fixed OZ units of Y and the cost of the number of units of X which minimizes unit cost. In estimating the cost of nuclear power it will therefore be necessary to select the number of units of the variable inputs which minimize the unit fuel cost.

It is instructive to observe how actual nuclear power plant design relates to the theory of production. The following description of the general approach to the design of a nuclear plant is taken, in the main, from a standard

22

nuclear engineering text.[9] We should remember that the condition for minimum cost of a given output is that marginal products due to the last dollar spent on every input must be equated.

Suppose that the power plant is chosen to be of the pressurized-water type. The fuel must be slightly enriched in uranium 235, and a decision must be made concerning the degree of enrichment and the chemical form. Next, a choice must be made among different fuel-element geometries, the two most common being cylindrical rods and flat plates. Furthermore,

extensive "parametric studies" are necessary before definite conclusions are reached even with regard to the preliminary design. In the parametric calculations, an attempt is made to estimate the effect on the total power cost of changing various parameters, e.g., fuel enrichment, shape, size, and number of fuel elements, nature and thickness of cladding, ratio of fuel to moderator, coolant temperatures and flow rate, pressure drop, etc. The selection of the optimum design is often rendered complicated by the interrelationships among the variables. Thus, the consequences of changing one parameter must be considered in the light of the effects on others.

The optimum degree of enrichment, from the overall economic standpoint, depends upon several factors; these include the size of the core, the operating thermal power, the moderator-to-fuel ratio, the diameter of the fuel elements, the nature of the cladding, the expected burnup of the elements, and fuel cycle costs. The conversion of uranium-238 into fissile plutonium-239 is involved in some of these factors and must be taken into consideration. Both low enrichment and high enrichment have their advantages and disadvantages, and the final choice will be determined by a parametric study of all the variables.[10]

It should be noted, in the description above, that *prices* of inputs are considered as given, while the physical quantities, or configurations, of inputs are varied to minimize cost. That the prices of inputs are equally important in influencing reactor design has been stressed by Philip Mullenbach:

Let us ask now what difference AEC prices may make in the direction of reactor development and the allocation — or, possibly, misallocation — of resources. The differences in practice are usually subtle, but a few obvious ones can be cited for illustrative purposes. The 4 percent use charge, for example, is so low as a rental charge that only a small penalty falls on reactor operators who may carry a large inventory of nuclear fuel. . . . The comparative advantage of using stainless steel clad fuel elements as against more costly zirconium clad fuel elements is influenced by the 4 percent use charge. The present low charge favors the less

9. Glasstone and Sesonske, chap. 12.
10. Ibid., pp. 666–667.

23

efficient stainless steel fuel element, which requires a greater amount of uranium-235 to provide the same amount of heat. The allocation of resources does not appear to be most economic, that is, least wasteful.[11]

Before proceeding with the analytics of fuel and capital costs, it should be instructive to point out typical magnitudes of those costs. Table 4–2 gives figures of 1.4–1.5 mills per kilowatt-hour as representative fuel costs (a breakdown of fuel cost by components is also given there). Typical magnitudes for capital cost are 2.1–2.2 mills per kilowatt-hour.[12]

Fuel cost. An understanding of the determination of minimum fuel cost is rendered difficult by the complexity because of the large number of variables. For an analytical tool, we must select only the most important variables. Figures 2–8 through 2–18 are presented as a step in this direction by describing the behavior of these variables in a typical fuel cycle. In the following figures, the fuel cost components are shown in as simple a manner as possible. Chapters 4 and 5 will examine each of these components in detail. The shapes of the figures in this analysis are representative of the results of those chapters.

Figure 2–8 depicts the production function of enriched uranium. Two inputs are required: natural uranium and units of separative work.[13] The isoquants shown are different levels of enrichment of a unit of uranium fuel. The isoquants can also be regarded as different levels of grams or uranium-235 per unit of uranium output. As before, the locus of tangencies between price ratios and isoquants defines the total cost function. Notice that an increase in the price of natural uranium, *ceteris paribus,* would shift the price ratio lines clockwise, thereby generating a new total cost function for enriched uranium. The total cost function determined in figure 2–8 is constructed in figure 2–9.

Figure 2–10 portrays the productivity of uranium, or the amount of energy obtainable in megawatt-days per kilogram of uranium fuel as a function of the degree of fuel enrichment. The determinants of this relationship are complex and can be affected by a number of factors. For example, the simple rearrangement of fuel elements in a reactor can shift the function upward. Reactivity limits and possible radiation damage play an important role in the shape of the relation. In general, for a given reactor, we will assume that

11. "Government Pricing and Civilian Reactor Technology," in Henry Jarrett, ed., *Science and Resources* (Baltimore: Johns Hopkins Press, 1959), p. 176.

12. In 1968 the AEC released a major study of the cost of producing power in light water plants in which the fuel cost of an 800-megawatt plant was given as 1.75 mills and the capital cost as 2.82 mills (U.S. Atomic Energy Commission, *The Current Status and Future Technical and Economic Potential of Light Water Reactors,* Report WASH-1082, March, 1968).

13. *Separative work* is a term used by the AEC to represent a combination of inputs, other than uranium, necessary in the enrichment process (electric power, overhead, etc.).

24

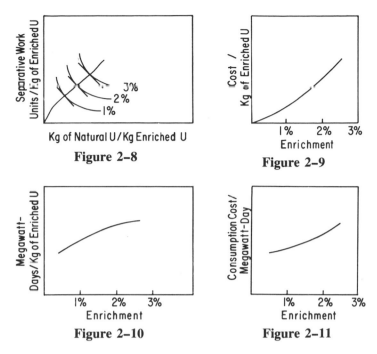

Figure 2-8

Figure 2-9

Figure 2-10

Figure 2-11

technology can specify energy output as an increasing function of enrichment.

The cost of fuel consumption is equal to the difference between the cost of the initial fuel charge minus the cost of the enriched uranium in the spent fuel. For simplicity, we will assume that the spent fuel contains enriched uranium of zero value.[14] Figure 2–11, the cost of fuel consumption versus fuel enrichment, is derived by dividing the ordinates in figure 2–9 by those in figure 2–10. The cost of fuel consumption per unit energy rises with increasing enrichment.[15]

Other basically independent cost elements of the fuel cycle are the costs of fabricating the fuel elements, reprocessing the spent fuel, and transporting the fuel. In chapter 5 we will consider the interdependence of these components and the enrichment levels when considered from the industry viewpoint. That is to say, economies of scale are important in these fuel

14. Since the enrichment of uranium in the spent fuel in our selected cycle can be considered as constant, independent of the enrichment of the fuel charge, the cost, or credit, for the spent fuel will be approximately constant. The subtraction of a constant value from the total cost function of uranium fuel does not change its curvature — the important point for this analysis.

15. Fuel costs are expressed in units of cost per megawatt-day. The unit, megawatt-day, is a measure of heat energy released in the reactor. Megawatt-days of heat energy could be converted into kilowatt-hours of electric energy by multiplying by a constant factor which takes account of the thermal efficiency of the power plant.

25

operations; and if all reactors should change from a low to a high enrichment the total *tons* of fuel required (for a given output of power) per unit time would decline. This is due, of course, to the relatively greater extraction of energy per ton from fuel of higher enrichment. But at this point we will consider these three costs to be independent of enrichment, as shown in figure 2–12. Dividing the ordinates of figure 2–12 by those of figure 2–10 to express the cost in per-unit-energy terms, we derive the decreasing cost curve of figure 2–13.

The working capital cost per unit energy is more complex. The need for fuel working capital arises from the fact that fuel must be bought and fabricated before it can be irradiated to produce revenue. The difference between the cash outflow and cash inflow is a function of many variables. As the level of enrichment increases, the energy extracted per unit of fuel rises, and therefore the fuel irradiation period increases, which makes the need for working capital greater. Also, the higher the enrichment level, the higher the cost of a unit of enriched uranium. Again, the working capital requirement will rise with increasing enrichment. There are other less significant variables which affect, both positively and negatively, the amount of working capital needed as enrichment increases, but these will be neglected for the present.

To convert the working capital cost into a cost per unit energy, we must divide by the energy per unit fuel. Both working capital cost and energy, on a per-unit-fuel basis, rise with increasing enrichment. Thus the resultant

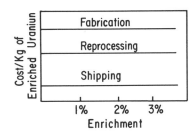

Figure 2–12

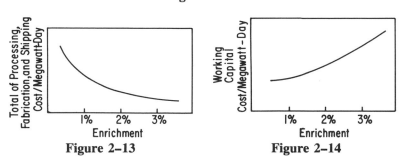

Figure 2–13 **Figure 2–14**

26

curve, working capital cost per unit energy as a function of enrichment, can have either a positive or a negative slope. Within the range of values which appear reasonable, the curve has a positive slope, as shown in figure 2–14.

At this juncture, we must recognize that energy is not the only output of our production function. In a nuclear power plant, electric energy is the primary output. However, the nuclear fission process also produces plutonium, a fact that we have ignored in our previous theory discussion. A small fraction of the plutonium is fissioned itself after being produced, but the remainder is recovered from the spent fuel and returned to the AEC. The AEC currently gives reactor operators a credit for plutonium, although in the future it is expected that a private demand for plutonium as a fuel will be established.

Electric energy and plutonium are therefore jointly produced outputs. All of the usual difficulties of cost measurement are present. Since the two outputs are jointly produced in variable proportions, it is theoretically possible to determine the marginal cost of each. The normal accounting approach to a joint cost problem is to follow some arbitrary allocation procedure. When one of the outputs is relatively unimportant an adequate procedure is to subtract the market value of the less important output from total cost to get the cost of the primary output. Since, in light water reactors, the credit for plutonium is on the order of only 15 percent of total fuel cost, we will follow the arbitrary practice discussed above.[16] Nevertheless, a change in the AEC price for plutonium will alter the optimum enrichment for minimum fuel cost.

Before indicating the subtractive effect of the plutonium credit, figure 2–15 shows the sum of all previously discussed cost components. The positively sloped fuel consumption and working capital cost functions (functions of enrichment) interact with the other negatively sloped cost functions to cause the total cost function to reach a minimum at some intermediate level of enrichment.

Figure 2–16 can be viewed either as a physical productivity of plutonium curve or as a plutonium credit curve (for a constant plutonium price). Figure 2–17 is obtained by dividing the ordinates of figure 2–16 by those of figure 2–10, thereby converting cost from a per-unit-fuel basis to a per-unit-energy basis. Figure 2–17 shows that a larger unit credit is obtainable at lower enrichments than at higher enrichments.

16. In advanced converters and breeder reactors the amount of plutonium (or uranium-233 in thorium-fueled reactors) produced is proportionately much greater than in light water reactors. However, the production functions of these advanced reactors can incorporate plutonium production into their formulation, thereby avoiding the joint cost problem. Plutonium can be viewed as an intermediate product since it can be used as fuel in the succeeding fuel cycle, which may also be possible soon in light water reactors with plutonium recycle technology.

The last chart, figure 2–18, demonstrates the effect of the plutonium credit on the total unit fuel cost. A major point to be gained from this simple analysis is that the level of enrichment is a key parameter of the fuel cycle. A change in almost any cost element makes it necessary to select a new level of enrichment for minimum fuel cost.

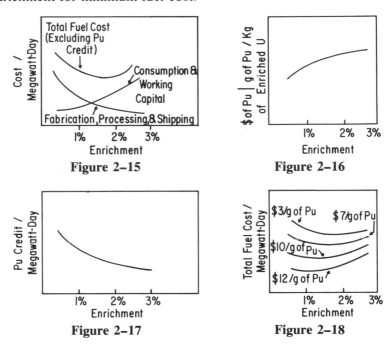

Figure 2–15

Figure 2–16

Figure 2–17

Figure 2–18

This graphic description of fuel cost determination was concerned with only one fuel cycle, the so-called equilibrium cycle. This cycle is the one during which "fuel-cycle operations have reached the 'steady-state' condition. For light water reactors, this point is usually reached during the life of the second core: four to eight years after plant startup."[17] For our benefit-cost analysis, the cost of the equilibrium cycle appears to be the appropriate one. We will compare fuel costs of light water and advanced converter reactors for each year of the analysis, and all reactors of the same type in a given year will be assumed to have the same equilibrium fuel cycle cost.

The more relevant fuel cycle cost concept for power companies is the lifetime fuel cost.[18] This approach is concerned with finding that constant amount of revenue per kilowatt-hour which is necessary to cover all fuel

17. *Nucleonics,* 22 (July 1964): 70.
18. For example, see the article in *Nucleonics,* 24 (January 1966): 40, by Paul Dragoumis et al., "Estimating Nuclear Fuel-Cycle Costs," which develops in detail this fuel cost concept.

costs over the plant lifetime. An expression for this cost can be derived as follows. Since the present value of revenues must equal the present value of costs,

$$\int_0^T f\, q(t)\, e^{-rt}\, dt = \int_0^T c(t)\, q(t)\, e^{-rt}\, dt \tag{2-10}$$

or

$$f = \frac{\displaystyle\int_0^T c(t)\, q(t)\, e^{-rt}\, dt}{\displaystyle\int_0^T q(t)\, e^{-rt}\, dt} \tag{2-11}$$

where f = revenue required per kilowatt-hour to cover fuel cost over plant lifetime

$c(t)$ = fuel cost at time t

$q(t)$ = kilowatt-hours produced at time t

e^{-rt} = the discount factor applicable to returns at time t with discount rate r

T = plant lifetime.

The lifetime unit fuel cost, f, is equal to the present value of all future fuel costs divided by all future units of output, also discounted. It can only be computed after first estimating fuel costs for each succeeding fuel cycle over the plant lifetime. The economics of fuel cost can be adequately treated within the framework of an equilibrium cycle analysis.

One other possible fuel cost concept should be mentioned. It is important at times to know the initial fuel cost. The initial fuel cost is "the projected cost over the first several years of plant operation, roughly corresponding to the cost experience anticipated for the first core."[19] For our purposes, the equilibrium fuel cycle cost is better because it gives a more representative figure of a cost which can be assigned to all reactors in a given year.

Capital cost. The cost of the nuclear power plant is a one-time cost, fixed over the plant life. The output of the plant takes place over a long period of time (relative to the shorter period of output associated with specific fuel inputs). It is a reasonable practice to allocate the cost of the plant over the time period during which output is produced. A constant plant, or capital, cost per unit of output over the life of the plant is an important figure for power companies. An expression for this unit cost, C, is given below.

The present value of revenues is equated to the present value of cost,

$$\int_0^T C\, q(t)\, e^{-rt}\, dt = K \tag{2-12}$$

19. *Nucleonics*, 22 (July 1964): 70.

or
$$C = \frac{K}{\displaystyle\int_{o}^{T} q(t)\, e^{-rt}\, dt} \qquad (2\text{-}13)$$

where
C = revenue required per kilowatt-hour to cover capital cost over plant lifetime

K = cost of nuclear power plant at time O

$q(t)$ = power generated at time t

e^{-rt} = the discount factor applicable to returns at time t with discount rate r

r = the discount rate, or the normal rate of return necessary to attract investment

T = plant lifetime.

The lifetime unit capital cost, C, is equal to the investment in the plant divided by the discounted quantity of all future output. One of the disadvantages of this formulation of capital cost is the difficulty in specifying the time path of output explicitly. One important factor to the output pattern is the "learning curve" or "stretch" effect. As experience is gained with a nuclear reactor, it is possible to increase significantly the output of the reactor. The output in the first few years may be increased by as much as 10–20 percent during the following years. The timing and amounts of these increases are of course important to the unit capital cost. Another factor affecting the time path of output is the rate of plant utilization, or plant factor.

A simpler and more popular expression for capital cost per unit of output is

$$C = \frac{(k)\,(FC)}{(8,760)\,(PF)} \qquad (2\text{-}14)$$

where
C = capital cost per kilowatt-hour

k = capital investment per kilowatt

FC = fixed charges, in percentage per year

PF = plant factor, in percentage (there are 8,760 possible operating hours per year).

The fixed-charges percentage represents the proportion of capital investment which must be recovered annually for depreciation and return on investment. Other fixed costs (such as insurance and property taxes) are also usually included as a part of fixed charges. That component of the fixed-charges percentage representing depreciation and return on investment, FC', can be calculated easily. Since

$$k = \int_{o}^{T} U e^{-rt}\, dt \qquad (2\text{-}15)$$

30

where k = capital investment per kilowatt

             U = payment required at time t to recover depreciation and return on investment

             r = normal rate of return on investment

             T — plant lifetime,

then

$$FC' = \frac{U}{k} = \frac{1}{\int_0^T e^{-rt}\,dt} = \frac{r}{1 - e^{-rt}}. \tag{2-16}$$

The discrete counterpart of equation 2–16 is given as equation 2–17 and can be found in any set of financial tables:

$$FC' = \frac{r}{1 - (1 + r)^{-T}}. \tag{2-17}$$

The plant factor is the percentage of total possible operating hours per year during which the plant is producing power. Plants normally operate at high plant factors during early years and low plant factors during later years. The reason is that when a plant is new its marginal cost is usually lower than other plants in the system. It will therefore be operated more hours than older plants with higher marginal costs. As a plant ages, it is continually being displaced by newer plants with lower marginal costs. Hence, in later years a particular plant's plant factor is likely to decline.

The expression for capital cost given in equation 2–14 is quite easy to use and is therefore popular. Its simplicity, however, also makes it somewhat dangerous. An implicit assumption is that capacity is constant, thus "stretch" is ignored. Furthermore, the selection of a particular value for plant factor requires much qualification. For example, the plant factor selected may be an "average lifetime" plant factor, or it may be a plant factor for the first five years. These problems will be discussed further in chapters 3 and 6.

For the benefit-cost analysis, the appropriate capital cost figure will be simply the cost per kilowatt of capacity. That is to say, in each year the calculation will be to subtract the initial capital cost of advanced converter reactors from the capital cost of light water reactors for the predicted kilowatts of capacity added in that year. However, in analyzing the investment decision of private firms it will be necessary to make use of the expressions discussed above. Moreover, since almost all firms operate more than one plant, the incremental capital cost to the system of plants is the relevant concept.

This chapter has only served as an introduction to the concepts of cost which will be employed in the succeeding four chapters. The first part of the chapter was presented to provide a minimum technical basis for understanding the cost of nuclear power.

Chapter 3. Capital Cost

The capital cost of a light water nuclear plant includes cost items for the site, nuclear reactor, turbine-generator, station design, installation, and interest during construction. Philip Sporn of the American Electric Power Company, an authority on electric utility economics, has estimated that the capital cost per kilowatt-hour for a January 1966 vintage, 800-megawatt nuclear plant is one-half of total production cost (fuel cost, the other major component, is 41 percent).[1]

For our benefit-cost analysis, the capital cost should be expressed per unit capacity rather than per unit output. Hence, here we shall not make use of the expressions for capital cost per unit of output derived in chapter 2. In chapter 6 we shall discuss the comparative costs of nuclear and non-nuclear plants in the context of the investment decision of the firm; there capital cost per unit of output will be relevant.

To illustrate the relative magnitude of each capital cost component, table 3–1 gives the Niagara Mohawk Power Company estimate for its Nine Mile Point plant. This plant was ordered in 1963 at the same time Jersey Central Power and Light Company ordered its well-known Oyster Creek plant (generally regarded as the first "commercial" nuclear plant in the United States). Both plants were ordered from General Electric and are of about the same capacity. Nine Mile Point is expected to have an initial net capacity of 500 megawatts with a stretch capacity of 620 megawatts, while the corresponding figures for Oyster Creek are 510 and 640.

Table 3–2 is an analysis of the large difference in total capital cost of the two plants: $22.2 million. The value of this comparison is that it sheds light upon the level of capital cost in 1963 and also, by example, emphasizes the problems involved in comparing capital costs of recently ordered plants.

One major difference between the two plants is the nature of the purchase contract. Oyster Creek was contracted on a turnkey basis: for a fixed price,

1. Philip Sporn, "Nuclear Power Economics: An Appraisal of the Current Technical-Economic Position of Nuclear and Conventional Generation," speech at Morgan Guaranty Hall, New York, March 1966, p. 24. Referred to hereafter as Sporn, 1966.

Table 3–1. Estimated capital cost of Nine Mile Point 500-megawatt nuclear plant

Item	Millions of dollars	Percentage
Direct costs		
Land	1.5	1.7
Site survey and preparation	0.6	0.7
Structures	11.0	12.2
Nuclear reactor	30.8	34.1
Turbine-generator	18.8	20.8
Accessory electrical equipment	2.0	2.2
Miscellaneous power plant	1.4	1.6
Switchyard	2.0	2.2
	68.0	75.3
Indirect costs		
Engineering	3.3	3.7
Construction engineer services	2.5	2.8
Distributable construction items	2.1	2.3
Taxes during construction	0.3	0.3
Personnel training	1.0	1.1
Interest during construction	6.0	6.7
	14.1	15.6
Contingency	4.5	5.0
Escalation	2.6	2.9
Grand total	90.2	100.0

Source: Nucleonics, 22 (May 1964): 17.

General Electric will supply and take responsibility for the complete plant up to the beginning of commercial power production. On the other hand, Niagara Mohawk will participate in plant design, construction, and subcontracting for plant components as its own architect-engineer.

After the adjustment made in table 3–2 to make total costs more comparable, there remains an apparent difference of $13.6 million.

Almost all this remaining difference can be broken down . . . into two major elements — deliberate conservatism in preparation of the direct cost estimates possibly amounting to $9 million, and further conservatism in the form of an allowance for contingencies that is $3.5 million higher than for Oyster Creek. In my judgement, there appears to be little doubt that when the two plants are completed, the final difference in

Table 3-2. Analysis of Oyster Creek and Nine Mile Point cost differences

	Millions of dollars
Oyster Creek, total capital cost	68.0
Difficult construction conditions at Nine Mile Point	5.0
Escalation (not included in Oyster Creek cost)	2.6
Higher land cost at Nine Mile Point	0.7
Higher interest during construction	0.7
Lower training cost at Nine Mile Point	(−0.4)
Total	76.6
Total cost for Oyster Creek, corrected for Nine Mile Point conditions	76.6
Total Nine Mile Point capital cost	90.2
Apparent difference	13.6

Sources: Philip Sporn, "A Post–Oyster Creek Evaluation of the Current Status of Nuclear Electric Generation," in *Nuclear Power Economics: Analysis and Comments, 1964,* prepared for the U.S. Congress, Joint Committee on Atomic Energy, October 1964, p. 9; and *Nucleonics,* 24 (March 1966): 17.

total cost will be substantially less than the current estimates would seem to indicate.[2]

Sporn is confident that

whatever cost differential may remain in favor of Oyster Creek does not represent an inherent cost penalty associated with Niagara Mohawk's participation . . . as its own architect-engineer as contrasted to the purchase of a turnkey job. The record shows that those utilities having the manpower and resources to support their own architect-engineering organizations, by incorporating their unique operating experience as a guide to new plant design, have been able to do an unexcelled job in putting together the most efficient and economical advanced conventional power plants. . . . The fact that an estimate for an initial utility engineered atomic unit is being made with considerably more conservatism than a manufacturer's turnkey estimate, may reflect the limited utility experience along these lines, but may also be due to nothing more than a matter of a particular management cost estimating philosophy.[3]

2. Philip Sporn, "A Post–Oyster Creek Evaluation of the Current Status of Nuclear Electric Generation," *Nuclear Power Economics: Analysis and Comments, 1964,* prepared for the U.S. Congress, Joint Committee on Atomic Energy, October 1964, p. 9. Referred to hereafter as Sporn, 1964.
3. Ibid.

Having raised the question of the uncertainty surrounding capital cost estimates, we should also introduce the problem of uncertainty in capacity estimates. The capacities of Oyster Creek and Nine Mile Point were described by two figures: the initial capacity and the stretch capacity. Stretch capacity refers to the ultimate capacity the plant is expected to attain by virtue of experience gained from operation. Since there has been very little operating experience with nuclear plants, stretch is currently a large item. "The Niagara Mohawk and Jersey Central plants allow for somewhat over 20 percent. The trend in future plants incorporating new advanced technology will undoubtedly be to lower levels of stretch."[4] This statement of a General Electric representative is true, at least with respect to estimates of stretch for the nuclear plants ordered more recently. Table 3–3 demonstrates this trend.[5]

Clearly, both the time required to achieve stretch and the amount of stretch are important economic factors. In order to compress both factors into a single capacity measure, we must calculate the constant lifetime capacity which is equivalent to a capacity which varies over its lifetime.

If we assume that the utility will be indifferent between two plants providing equal present values of lifetime revenues and that the price of output is constant, equation 3–1 permits us to derive an expression for K, the desired single-capacity measure. We will also make the assumption that capacity increases linearly with time until stretch is attained.

$$\int_0^T K e^{-rt} \, dt = \int_0^h [I + \frac{t}{h}(U - I)]e^{-rt} \, dt + \int_h^T U e^{-rt} \, dt \qquad (3-1)$$

where
K = equivalent constant lifetime capacity
I = initial capacity
U = stretch capacity
h = time to achieve stretch
T = life of plant
r = discount rate.

Integrating, and solving for K, gives

$$K = \frac{I + \dfrac{U - I}{rh}(1 - e^{-rh}) - U e^{-rT}}{1 - e^{-rT}}. \qquad (3-2)$$

4. G. J. Stathakis, "Nuclear Power Drives Energy Costs Down," *Electrical World*, 5 October 1964.

5. General Electric has recently stopped the policy of selling nuclear plants "at two or even three ratings. . . . GE will make proposals only on the basis of the turbine nameplate rating" (*Nucleonics*, 24 [July 1966]: 23). Hence, we have not included the latest GE sale (2,129-megawatt plant to TVA in June 1966) in table 3–3. Also, a July 1966 Babcock and Wilcox sale to Duke Power is omitted for lack of stretch estimates.

Table 3–3. Stretch estimates for nuclear plants

Plant	Location	Order date	Initial megawatts	Stretch megawatts	Percentage stretch
San Onofre	Calif.	1963	395	450	14
Haddam Neck	Conn.	1963	462	562	22
Oyster Creek	N.J.	1963	510	640	25
Nine Mile Point	N.Y.	1963	500	620	24
Malibu	Calif.	1963	462	562	22
Dresden-2	Ill.	1965	715	793	11
Boston	Mass.	1965	540	612	13
Brookwood	N.Y.	1965	420	450	7
Millstone Point	Conn.	1965	549	650	18
Indian Point-2	N.Y.	1965	873	983	13
Turkey Point-3	Fla.	1965	691	721	4
Dresden-3	Ill.	1966	715	793	11
Hartsville	S.C.	1966	663	731	10
Palisades	Mich.	1966	710	810	14
Wisconsin Power	Wis.	1966	454	480	6
Cordova	Ill.	1966	715	809	13
Monticello	Minn.	1966	472	545	15

Source: *Nucleonics*, 24 (March 1966): 17; and 24 (May 1966): 26.

As an example, we will make the following assumptions for Oyster Creek:

$$I = 510 \text{ megawatts}$$
$$U = 640 \text{ megawatts}$$
$$h = 3 \text{ years}$$
$$T = 30 \text{ years}$$
$$r = .06.$$

If Oyster Creek attains stretch capacity three years from start-up, equivalent capacity, K, is 627 megawatts. For a longer interval, or h, the equivalent capacity is lower. Thus, if h is seven years, K is only 611 megawatts. The respective Oyster Creek capital costs per kilowatt for these two capacities are $108 and $111.

If we follow Sporn in believing that a stretch of 25 percent is too optimistic for Oyster Creek[6] — apparently substantiated by stretch estimates for more recent plants (see table 3–3) — we can recalculate the equivalent capacities for a smaller stretch, say 10 percent. The capacity for an h of

6. Sporn, 1964, p. 7.

three years then becomes 556 megawatts, and 550 megawatts for an *h* of seven years. The respective costs per kilowatt are $122 and $124.

The use of thirty years for the assumed lifetime can only be an estimate. Although it is now common to take this to be thirty years, there is no real basis for doing so. The estimate of *h* is similarly unfounded. Only when some operating experience is gained can better estimates be had.

Following a brief analysis of the nuclear plant market structure, we will use the formulation above to study recent nuclear plant capital costs. Finally, we will make a capital cost prediction for use in the benefit-cost analysis.

Nuclear Plant Market Structure[7]

Table 3–4 shows the relative shares of light water nuclear plant suppliers in both the domestic and the world markets. The total megawatts supplied include all plants in operation or ordered through March 1966 (as

Table 3–4. Orders of light water nuclear plants, by suppliers

Supplier	United States		World	
	Megawatts	Percentage	Megawatts	Percentage
Allis-Chalmers[a]	131	1.2	131	0.9
Babcock and Wilcox	255	2.3	255	1.7
Cumbustion Engineering	727	6.6	727	4.7
General Electric	4,259	38.6	5,843	37.9
Westinghouse	5,651	51.3	6,938	45.0
AEG (Germany)			201	1.3
ASEA (Sweden)			400	2.6
Siemens (Germany)			282	1.8
USSR			633	4.1
Totals	11,023	100.0	15,410	100.0

[a]Withdrew as nuclear plant supplier in March 1966.

Note: A more recent list of the percentages for the United States market (as of September 1969) is: Babcock and Wilcox, 13; Combustion Engineering, 7; General Electric, 38; and Westinghouse, 33 (U.S. Atomic Energy Commission, *The Nuclear Industry,* 1969, December 1969, p. 134).

Source: Nuclear Engineering, April 1966.

reported in April 1966 issue of *Nuclear Engineering*). Clearly, both the number of firms and the inequality of shares is great. If we include all types of reactors, the dominance of General Electric and Westinghouse in the world market is reduced considerably — as shown in table 3–5.

7. A thorough study of the nuclear market was prepared by Arthur D. Little, Inc., in 1968 for the AEC and the Department of Justice. See *Competition in the Nuclear Power Supply Industry,* December 1968.

Table 3–5. Orders of all nuclear plants, by suppliers

Supplier	Megawatts	Percentage
Allis-Chalmers[a]	131	0.4
Babcock and Wilcox	255	0.7
Combustion Engineering	727	2.0
General Electric	6,546	17.6
Westinghouse	6,938	18.7
Ontario Hydro	1,212	3.3
France	2,447	6.6
Finland	300	0.8
Germany	674	1.8
Sweden	532	1.4
United Kingdom	14,765	39.6
USSR	1,882	5.0
Totals	37,119	100.0

[a]Withdrew as nuclear plant supplier in March 1966.
Source: Nuclear Engineering, April 1966.

External economies resulting from the government's $2.3 billion World War II investment in uranium enrichment facilities is an important factor in the predominance of light water reactors in this country. Although it is possible that foreign-sponsored reactors may gain a share of the domestic market in the future, we shall explore that possibility only briefly here.

Most foreign-sponsored reactors have been fueled with natural uranium (owing mainly to the desire to be independent of the United States as the supplier of enriched uranium), but in recent, well-publicized competition to supply the reactors for the second British nuclear power program, a British consortium, offering an advanced gas-cooled reactor fueled with slightly enriched uranium, was awarded the contract over a General Electric boiling water reactor. There was considerable controversy over the validity of the comparative cost analysis and some doubt whether General Electric's bid was as low as it could have been.[8] Nevertheless, we should not exclude the possibility of such competition in this country.

8. The first striking feature of the [comparative cost analysis] is that the bid quotation for the BWR's— . . . more than $168 per kilowatt for the 1,048 mw station—is extremely high compared to GE's published prices for nuclear plants built for U.S. utilities. . . . Even assuming that the best price a U.S. purchaser could get for the two-plant installation would be twice the price list quotation for a single 550 mw plant, he would still come out approximately $30 million ahead of the quotation cited in the . . . analysis and would have an extra 50 mw of capacity. . . . Most observers have assumed that . . . the gap can only be attributed to the higher costs of the components manufactured in England and higher construction costs. (*Nuclear Industry,* August 1965, p. 11).
For more details see the official report by the United Kingdom's Central Electricity Generating Board, *An Appraisal of the Technical and Economic Aspects of Dungeness B Nuclear Power Station,* 1965. Also *Nucleonics,* 23 (September 1965): 25.

With the exception of but two or three of the plants listed in table 3-3, all nuclear plants have been contracted on a turnkey basis. Since Combustion Engineering will not bid on a turnkey basis[9] and Allis-Chalmers has announced its withdrawal from the nuclear reactor business,[10] nuclear plant supply is even more highly concentrated than is indicated in table 3-4. Two other reactor suppliers not listed in table 3-4, Atomics International and General Atomics, have dropped from active competition in light water reactors and are concentrating on advanced converters. General Electric and Westinghouse appear to be an even more effective duopoly when it is recognized that the only other turnkey supplier—Babcock and Wilcox— must buy the turbine-generator unit of the nuclear plant from General Electric or Westinghouse.

An argument is underway that GE and Westinghouse "shave" the price of electrical parts of the plant, as they make all the pieces. The contention is that Babcock and Wilcox must pay the price set by the electrical companies, plus their profits, when it buys a turbine-generator for a turnkey bid but that the makers can include the generator in their bids at cost.[11]

The domination of supply by two firms has reportedly so disturbed the AEC that it has

"informally" approached the Justice Department's antitrust division. Among the thoughts explored: setting up a policy that would encourage mergers between the weaker atomic equipment suppliers.[12]

The current situation is partially a result of past policies followed by the AEC in developing nuclear technology.

Information in the form of industrial know-how was obtained long before the 1954 revision of atomic energy legislation by AEC contractors who were gaining experience in technology now assuming commercial importance.[13]

Westinghouse and General Electric held all contracts in the naval reactor development program until a contract for a small submarine reactor was awarded to Combustion Engineering in August 1955.[14]

Also, there are a number of barriers which tend to restrict entry into the nuclear reactor supply industry. A large capital investment is required, and

9. *Wall Street Journal,* 31 January 1966, p. 2.
10. *New York Times,* 26 March 1966, p. 35.
11. Ibid., 31 January 1966, p. 2.
12. Ibid., 21 January 1966, p. 1.
13. Richard Tybout, *The Reactor Supply Industry,* (Columbus, Ohio: Bureau of Business Research, Ohio State University, 1960), p. 3.
14. Morgan Thomas, "Democratic Control of Atomic Power Development," *Law and Contemporary Problems,* 21 (1956): 49.

the technology is complex. Patents have been unimportant insofar as the AEC has made the technology generally "well known and broadly available."[15] Another barrier is the long-standing relationship with utilities which suppliers in the conventional power plant industry have been able to carry over into the nuclear industry.

Turning to the demand side of the market, we find the electrical utilities, each with a regional monopoly. Their demand for capital equipment is derived from the demand for electricity. In the long run, the demand for power plants may be inelastic to price, "but the flexibility they have in the timing of their purchases, combined with the size of the increment gives them real leverage in the market."[16]

The present high degree of competitiveness between nuclear and non-nuclear plants should tend to make the demand curve facing a nuclear plant supplier more elastic, and similarly for a nonnuclear supplier. However, as pointed out earlier, in addition to their duopoly in nuclear plants General Electric and Westinghouse also have a duopoly in turbine-generators, a large component of nuclear and nonnuclear plants. The dichotomy of nuclear and nonnuclear suppliers is more apparent than real.

Of course, the important issue for an efficient allocation of resources is the relation of market price to marginal cost. Although as yet there is no way to predict the performance of a market from its structural characteristics, "as a general statistical matter, the greater the concentration the lower the odds in favor of competitive behavior."[17]

The history of the past few decades of the electrical equipment industry should make one pessimistic on this score. For example, since 1940 General Electric and Westinghouse have been involved in no less than twelve separate antitrust cases.[18] The last and most infamous has been the subject of a number of books and a congressional investigation.[19] In this 1960 electrical equipment case, twenty-nine manufacturers were indicted on charges of price fixing, bid rigging, and market splitting.[20] The case came to light in 1958 when

15. Francis K. McCune, "The Impact of Government Regulation on Technological Development in Nuclear Energy," in Edward J. Bloustein, ed., *Nuclear Energy, Public Policy, and the Law* (Dobbs Ferry, N.Y.: Oceana, 1964), p. 25.

16. C. Walton and F. Cleveland, *Corporations on Trial: The Electric Cases* (Belmont, Calif.: Wadsworth, 1964), p. 23.

17. Statement of M. A. Adelman in Hearings on *Economic Concentration, Part I*, U.S. Senate Subcommittee on Antitrust and Monopoly, July and September 1964, p. 230.

18. Walton and Cleveland, pp. 18, 19.

19. John Fuller, *The Gentlemen Conspirators* (New York: Grove Press, 1962); John Herling, *The Great Price Conspiracy* (Washington: Robert B. Luce, 1962); U.S. Senate Committee on the Judiciary, Subcommittee on Antitrust and Monopoly, Hearings on Administered Prices, *Price-Fixing and Bid-Rigging in the Electrical Manufacturing Industry*, Parts 27 and 28, April, May, and June 1961.

20. Walton and Cleveland, p. 33.

the TVA, preparing to ask for bids on the steam turbine-generators for its new plant, became disturbed over the very rapid increase in steam turbine-generator prices. . . . The TVA decided to invite bids from foreign manufacturers . . . in an effort to secure lower prices. On February 6, 1959, the TVA announced the award of a contract to . . . an English firm . . . at a price of $12,095,800. Almost immediately General Electric announced that it would protest the award. Shortly thereafter, Westinghouse made a similar announcement. The companies argued that such an award would be detrimental to the national security. . . . The TVA rejected the arguments and added the further comment that the [English firm's] bid was more than $6 million below the bids of General Electric and Westinghouse.[21]

If utilities should return to nonturnkey contracting for nuclear plants, a continuing competitive behavior would become more probable. As *Electrical World* has editorialized,

> rejection of turnkey contracts would strengthen the position of established reactor builders of limited capitalization who do not manufacture electrical equipment . . . and dilute the very real threat that continued adherence to the turnkey concept may force two or three strong reactor builders to withdraw from the market-place.[22]

The announcement in January 1966 by Consumers Power Company that it "would depart from general industry practice and buy parts for [its new 700-megawatt] nuclear plant from several suppliers"[23] may indicate the beginning of a movement toward nonturnkey contracting.[24]

Price Data

To relate price data for plants of different capacities, we must understand that economies of scale are important. These economies are due to certain technological relationships which permit capacity to increase faster than inputs. Consequently, cost does not increase proportionally to capacity.

> The savings in capital cost comes about because some items of plant investment are relatively independent of size, for instance site development, plant buildings, and overhead items such as engineering design costs.
>   The reactor instrumentation and control system, reactor containment,

21. Ibid., pp. 29–30.
22. *Electrical World*, 10 January 1966, p. 7.
23. *New York Times*, 29 January 1966, p. 31.
24. After this analysis was completed, General Electric announced that it was abandoning the turnkey method of selling nuclear plants in the United States. GE stated that it wished to return to its "historic role as a systems manufacturer and to get out of the construction business" (*New York Times*, 15 June 1966, p. 62).

41

shielding, water disposal, and fuel-handling systems are some of the plant components that do not increase in proportion to unit size.[25]

Table 3–6, based on a manufacturer's price handbook, demonstrates the economies of scale in capital equipment.[26] The largest unit for which prices are available is a 1,000-megawatt unit (the assumed size for our benefit-cost analysis). The capital cost per kilowatt for the 1,000-megawatt plant is only 34 percent of the cost of a 50-megawatt plant and 82 percent of the cost of a 500-megawatt unit.

Table 3–6. Manufacturer's handbook price for nuclear plants

Plant rating (megawatts)	50	250	500	750	1,000
Plant price (dollars per kilowatt)	314	169	131	115	107
Owner costs (dollars per kilowatt)	47	25	19	17	16
Total capital cost (dollars per kilowatt)	361	194	150	132	123
Total cost per kilowatt as a percentage of total cost per kilowatt of 50-megawatt plant	100	54	42	37	34

Note: The Atomic Energy Commission has estimated that the total capital cost of a 1,000-megawatt plant (as of 1969) has increased to nearly $200 per kilowatt (*The Nuclear Industry, 1969*, p. 129).

Source: W. A. Chittenden, "Nuclear or Fossil: How Do You Choose?" *Electrical World,* 2 May 1966, p. 74.

Although cost estimates for plants greater than 1,000 megawatts are not available, a priori one might expect that unit capital costs could decrease still more, though at a slower rate, with further capacity increases.[27] It is therefore interesting to consider what constraints, if any, will ultimately limit exploitation of economies of scale.

25. Harold L. Davis, "How Big Will Power Plants Get?" *Nucleonics,* 21 (June 1963): 60.
26. The handbook prices are not equivalent to actual ones, but relative handbook prices are sufficient to indicate scale economies in equipment manufacturing, and hence, also in electric power production. Actual prices are currently somewhat less: "this [handbook price] needs to be adjusted to a negotiated price to make it more comparable with the discount off handbook price which Dresden-2 apparently enjoyed" (Sporn, 1966, pp. 15–16).
27. In a recent contract announcement (June 1966) the Tennessee Valley Authority is reported to have a capital cost of only $117 per kilowatt for two 1,065-megawatt units. This is lower than our estimate ($120) for a 1,000-megawatt plant, but part of the lower cost may be due to the fact that there are two units and that TVA uses a low 4.5 percent interest rate.

Examination of the factors that could limit plant size leads us to the conclusion that coal-fired plants will be limited to outputs of perhaps 5,000 megawatts by problems of air pollution and a growing scarcity of cooling-water supply in the low-cost coal regions. In contrast, nuclear plants will not be subject to these limitations imposed by siting, and ultimately may be limited in size only by system-reliability considerations.[28]

Most capital costs announced by utilities for new nuclear plants are not itemized. In fact, it is not even possible in many instances to know whether the figure represents the turnkey price alone or the turnkey price plus owner's costs. Based upon recently released information, Philip Sporn has made an analysis of the Dresden-2 plant ordered in February 1965. This provides us with a good estimate of the capital cost of a nuclear plant more advanced than Oyster Creek or Nine Mile Point.

Using Sporn's Dresden-2 cost adjustments, we have adjusted capital costs, as appropriate, of the other nuclear plants which have been ordered through mid-1966. Although subsequent utility releases of cost breakdowns may prove our adjustments to be wrong, the adjusted costs in table 3–7 agree reasonably well with Sporn's estimate in table 3–8. The difference between Sporn's estimate for Dresden-2 and our estimate for the same plant is due to our use of a lower capacity figure. Sporn assumed that stretch will be attained upon start-up.

Each of the observations is plotted in figure 3–1. The capacities were calculated on the basis of a three-year stretch period, and the curve represents the manufacturer's handbook prices given in table 3–6.

Part of the reason for the relatively lower unit capital cost of Oyster Creek (*OC* in figure 3–1) has already been ascribed to the cost estimating philosophy of the owning utility. In addition, Sporn has pointed to the high degree of competition prevailing between General Electric and Westinghouse prior to the Oyster Creek award. General Electric was especially anxious to win the Oyster Creek contract in view of the fact that Westinghouse had been selected to supply each of the three preceding plants: San Onofre, Malibu, and Haddam Neck.

> Given this intense competitive background, the opportunity to bid for a nuclear plant at Oyster Creek called forth the effort to incorporate in one project simultaneously every available technological development, and every optimistic market projection based upon the new pricings

---

28. Davis, p. 60. A plant ten times larger than another must have components which are ten times as reliable as the smaller plant's components in order to have the same predicted downtimes. For example, a single jammed control rod might shut down a large plant as easily as a small one.

Table 3–7. Unit capital costs of light water nuclear plants ordered through mid-1966

Plant	Plant supplier	Start operation	Adjusted capital cost in millions of dollars	Stretch interval of three years[a]		Stretch interval of seven years[b]	
				Megawatts	Dollars per kilowatt	Megawatts	Dollars per kilowatt
San Onofre	Westinghouse	5/67	87.0[b]	444	196	438	199
Haddam Neck	Westinghouse	10/67	88.3[b]	552	160	540	164
Oyster Creek	General Electric	5/67	68.0[b]	627	108	611	111
Nine Mile Point	General Electric	11/68	90.2[b]	608	148	594	152
Malibu	Westinghouse	9/68	92.5[b]	552	167	540	171
Dresden-2	General Electric	2/69	94.8[c]	785	121	776	122
Brookwood	Westinghouse	6/69	74.3[d]	447	166	443	168
Millstone Point	General Electric	8/69	83.0[e]	640	130	628	132
Indian Point-2	Westinghouse	4/69	111.2[f]	972	114	959	116
Turkey Point-3	Westinghouse	4/69	87.7[g]	718	122	714	123
Dresden-3	General Electric	2/70	98.3[c]	785	125	776	127
Hartsville	Westinghouse	5/70	90.0[h]	724	124	716	126
Palisades	Combustion Engineering	4/70	104.0[i]	800	130	788	132
Wisconsin Power	Westinghouse	2/70	72.5[h]	477	152	474	153
Cordova	General Electric	3/70	95.6[h]	800	120	789	121
Monticello	General Electric	5/70	90.0[h]	538	167	528	170
TVA[j]	General Electric	1970	249.2[k]	2–1,065	117	–	–
Lake Keowee[j]	Babcock and Wilcox	1971	185.0[h]	2–790	117	–	–

[a] Equivalent capacity calculations assume a life of thirty years and a discount rate of 6 percent.

[b] Total costs given in *Electrical World*, 14 June 1965.

[c] Estimated by Philip Sporn (table 3–8).

[d] Total costs given in *Nuclear Industry*, February 1966.

[e] Total costs given in *Nuclear Industry*, March 1966.

[f] Total costs given in *Nucleonics*, 24 (January 1966): 26; $3.2 million added to adjust for nonvirgin site.

[g] Fuel core valued at $12.3 million subtracted from total cost given in *Wall Street Journal*, 16 November 1965.

[h] Added $2.5 million for switchyard and 16 percent for indirect costs.

[i] Fuel core valued at $12.6 million subtracted, then adjust as in note h.

[j] Most recent contracts, stretch estimates not available. Ultimate capacity of 1,644 megawatts for Duke Power's Lake Keowee plant was adjusted to 1,580 megawatts.

[k] Total costs given in TVA report, "Comparison of Coal-Fired and Nuclear Power Plants for TVA System," as quoted in National Coal Association Memorandum of 28 June 1966, p. 2.

Sources: Nucleonics, 24 (March 1966): 17; 5 (May 1966): 26; 7 (July 1966): 23; and *New York Times*, 6 July 1966, p. 2.

Table 3–8. Sporn estimate of capital cost of 800-megawatt, January 1966 vintage nuclear plant

	Millions of dollars
Capital cost of Dresden-2 plant, order in February 1965	75.3
Adjustment for virgin site (Dresden-2 benefits from existing nuclear plant at same site)	3.2
Switchyard	2.5
Other direct costs	0.8
Indirect cost at 16 percent	13.0
Grand total	94.8

Unit capital cost: $\dfrac{94,800,000}{800,000} = \$118$ per kilowatt

Adjustment for 4 percent upward revision of price in September 1965	$ 5 per kilowatt
Adjusted capital cost	$123 per kilowatt

Source: Philip Sporn, "Nuclear Power Economics: An Appraisal of the Current Technical-Economic Position of Nuclear and Conventional Generation," speech at Morgan Guaranty Hall, New York, March 1966, p. 14.

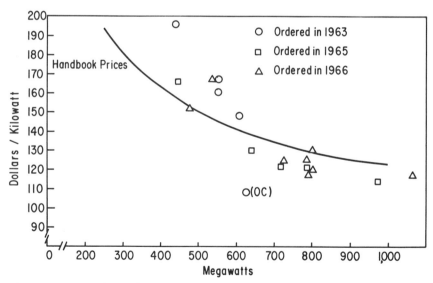

Figure 3–1. Unit capital costs versus capacity for light water nuclear plants in the United States

made possible by these developments, none of which however, had passed the test of experience. This is not to say that each of these developments do not have behind it creative engineering and sound technical foundations, but none is so striking or vital a departure from previous line of development to merit the term "breakthrough." Furthermore, it is generally known that GE priced Oyster Creek on the altogether reasonable assumption that three or more very similar units could be sold to minimize the financial risk of this particular plant. With all the good will toward all the organizations involved in the Oyster Creek project, it is still my personal judgment that one of the effects of the competitive pressures of the marketplace was to induce the manufacturer to risk somewhat greater uncertainty than might be tolerable repeatedly.[29]

Generally, the unit capital costs of the other large nuclear plants appear to follow a pattern which is similar to the curve of handbook prices. Most of the unit costs for large plants fall below the handbook curve, indicating that discounts have been given.

Of course it is hazardous to predict the unit capital costs of 1,000-megawatt plants for the next few years, and much more so for 1975 and 1985. Nevertheless, such predictions are necessary for the benefit-cost model. We shall make our predictions based upon the assumptions that current prices are near marginal costs and that our data accurately represent the total cost estimates of the utilities. Hence, a figure of $120 per kilowatt will be selected for 1975.[30] Clearly, uncertainty extends in both directions, and $120 is simply our subjective choice of the mean of the probability distribution. Our estimate for 1985 will be $110, based upon the expectation that the greater manufacturing experience by that date will lead to cost-reducing innovations.[31]

29. Sporn, 1964, p. 5.
30. In a 1968 report, Sporn stated that capital costs had risen to $140–$150 per kilowatt for a 1,000-megawatt plant. See U.S. Congress, Joint Committee on Atomic Energy, *Nuclear Power Economics, 1962–1967,* Febraury 1968.
31. An independent estimate by Arthur D. Little, Inc., of $100–$125 per kilowatt for a 1,000-megawatt plant in 1980 lends some support to our predictions (Arthur D. Little, Inc., *The Outlook for Central-Station Nuclear Power in the United States,* September 1964, p. 21).

Chapter 4. Nuclear Fuel Cost: Consumption

The nuclear fuel cycle was discussed briefly in the preceding chapter, but since this chapter and the next will be concerned with a detailed analysis of the fuel cost of light water nuclear plants, it is necessary to develop that description further. Following the description, we shall examine the assumptions made in the fuel cost computer program which will be used in studying fuel cost. This program enables us to analyze the sensitivity of total fuel cost to changes in certain key parameters.

Figure 4–1 is a schematic drawing of the steps in the fuel cycle. The first step is mining of the uranium ore. After it is mined the ore goes to mills where it is reduced to the concentrate, U_3O_8. From the mills, the U_3O_8 is sent to facilities for conversion to uranium hexafluoride, UF_6. Natural uranium in the form of UF_6 is required as the input to the AEC gaseous diffusion plants. The natural uranium input for a diffusion plant is slightly enriched in uranium-235 concentration.

It is at this point that the term *fuel cycle* becomes accurate. As figure 4–1 shows, there is a circular flow of the enriched uranium from the enrichment plant, to the fabrication plant, on to the reactor for irradiation then to the reprocessing plant, and back to the diffusion plant.

The importance of the government in the cost of nuclear fuel can also be seen in figure 4–1. The main function performed by the AEC is enrichment, although the plutonium credit is also an important factor subject to government policy.

Prior to the passage of the Private Fuels Ownership Bill in August 1964 the government was an even more important influence in the nuclear fuel cycle.[1] Reactor operators could lease but not own special nuclear materials. The low lease rate, 4.75 percent of the inventory value per year, is clearly a subsidy, and the law established a schedule for ending it. Private fuels ownership was legalized immediately, although few reactor operators will exercise the option while leasing is still possible. The AEC will make toll-enrichment services available in 1969. Operators who can obtain fuel at

---

1. The provisions of the bill are summarized in *Nucleonics,* 22 (September 1964): 17.

lower cost by buying natural uranium and having it toll-enriched will forego leasing after 1969. January 1971 is the terminal date for the leasing option, a date which will also mark the end of the guaranteed government buying price for plutonium. Since the benefits with which we are concerned should

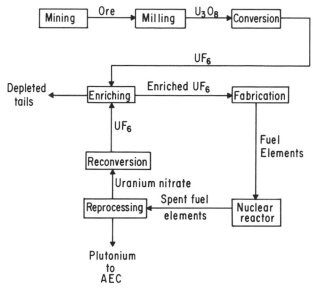

Figure 4–1. The nuclear fuel cycle

occur in the period after 1971, we shall assume in the following analysis that private ownership prevails completely.

It will be helpful to express the total fuel cost algebraically:

$$\frac{\text{Fuel cost}}{\text{(mills per kwh)}} = \frac{C + F + R + S + WC - P}{XE}$$

where

C = cost of fuel consumed per kilogram of fuel
F = fabrication cost per kilogram of fuel
R = reprocessing cost per kilogram of fuel
S = shipping cost per kilogram of fuel
WC = working capital cost per kilogram of fuel
P = plutonium credit per kilogram of fuel
X = exposure in kilowatt-hours of heat energy released per kilogram of fuel
E = thermal efficiency of plant (percentage of heat energy transformed into electric energy).

49

While this expression does point out the main components of cost, it unfortunately obscures some important interrelations. For example, the important effect of the level of fuel enrichment, shown graphically in chapter 2, is not apparent in the expression given above. It is clear that fuel cost can be reduced by increasing X, the exposure. Exposure can be increased by various means, but the most obvious is to raise the level of enrichment. However, a higher level of enrichment also means a higher cost for enriched uranium, which increases the consumption cost, C, and also increases the cost of working capital, WC. As a result of these interdependencies, it is necessary to devise a method for analyzing the sensitivity of fuel cost to changes in key inputs. For this purpose, a computer program will be used.

Basically, the computer program follows the calculaton procedure shown graphically in figures 2–8 through 2–18 in chapter 2. All costs are computed as functions of fuel enrichment. Total fuel cost as a function of enrichment is convex; it therefore reaches a minimum at some intermediate enrichment. Thus, for each value of a parameter being varied, total fuel cost must be minimized with respect to enrichment.

Certain physics characteristics of a light water reactor had to be assumed to construct a fuel cost program. The January 1965 ORNL report, discussed previously, provides such physics data for a 1,000-megawatt pres-

Table 4–1. Physics data assumed in fuel cost computer program

Feed enrichment in equilibrium cycle, wt. percentage U-235	1.696	2.198	2.656	2.938	3.271	3.662
Exposure, megawatt-days per kilogram of uranium	13.1	21.1	27.6	31.4	35.8	40.7
Discharge enrichment, wt. percentage U-235	0.651	0.630	0.592	0.592	0.597	0.608
Fuel lifetime, full-power days	417	670	880	1,002	1,141	1,300
Feed, thousands of kilograms of uranium	34.4	34.6	34.8	34.9	35.0	35.1
Fissile plutonium, thousands of kilograms discharged	0.126	0.152	0.169	0.177	0.186	0.195

Source: M. W. Rosenthal et al., *A Comparative Evaluation of Advanced Converters*, AEC Research and Development Report ORNL-3686, January 1965, pp. 154, 187.

surized water nuclear plant.[2] The data were originally submitted by Westinghouse to the AEC, and the AEC revised the data, as necessary, based upon its own research. Table 4–1 gives the data used in the program.

The important relation between exposure and enrichment was approximated by an equation of the form $Y = \alpha + \beta \ln X$, with ordinary least-squares techniques. Although only six data points are shown in table 4–1, additional data points were obtained by approximation from a graph of the relation in the ORNL report.[3] The resulting equation, exposure (megawatt-days per kilogram) $= 161.75 + 36.80 \ln$ (enrichment), has a coefficient of determination of 0.994.

We shall now begin detailed analyses of each of the components of fuel cost. This chapter will be devoted to consumption cost, and chapter 5 will consider the remaining costs.

Consumption

The cost of fuel consumed per kilowatt-hour of electricity amounts to slightly over half of total fuel cost. Before proceeding further, it may be helpful to examine table 4–2, which is presented to illustrate the relative magnitudes of the various components of fuel cost for physics data assumed in the computer program and of the cost assumptions given at the bottom of the table. Clearly, consumption is a large fraction of total cost.

There are three main factors which determine consumption cost: reactor physics, price of natural uranium, and cost of enrichment. The price of natural uranium will be the subject of chapter 6. Here, we shall vary the price over a reasonable range to examine its impact on cost.

We have assumed the reactor to have the physics characteristics of the 1,000-megawatt pressurized water reactor in the ORNL study. At this point, however, it is instructive to observe the mass balance around the reactor shown in figure 4–2. The formula for the cost of consumption is easy to derive from the figure.

$$C = 1.0 \, (P_{2.2}) - 0.971 \, (P_{0.6}) \qquad (4-1)$$

where
$\qquad C = $ cost of consumption per kilogram of fuel

$\qquad P_X = $ cost of 1.0 kilogram of uranium enriched at X percent.

Notice that the coefficient, 0.971, is not a constant for all calculations. The amount of uranium discharged from the reactor per kilogram of feed depends upon the design, fuel enrichment, and exposure. Following the

2. Rosenthal report, passim.
3. Ibid., p. 153.

Table 4–2. Illustrative fuel costs in mills per kilowatt-hour for 1,000-megawatt pressurized water reactor plant

Enrichment (percentage U-235)	Total	C	F	R	S	WC	P
2.25	1.46	.85	.33	.20	.03	.25	.19
	(100)	(58)	(22)	(13)	(2)	(17)	(−13)
2.50	1.44	.85	.29	.19	.03	.26	.17
	(100)	(59)	(20)	(13)	(2)	(18)	(−12)
2.75	1.44	.86	.27	.18	.02	.27	.15
	(100)	(59)	(18)	(13)	(2)	(19)	(−11)
3.00	1.46	.87	.25	.18	.02	.29	.15
	(100)	(60)	(17)	(12)	(1)	(20)	(−10)
3.25	1.49	.90	.23	.17	.02	.31	.14
	(100)	(60)	(16)	(12)	(1)	(21)	(−9)
3.50	1.53	.92	.22	.17	.02	.34	.13
	(100)	(60)	(15)	(11)	(1)	(22)	(−9)

Note: Percentages are given in parentheses; C = consumption, F = fabrication, R = reprocessing, S = shipping, WC = working capital, P = plutonium credit.

Assumptions: Natural uranium, $6 per pound of U_3O_8; separative work cost, $30 per kilogram; plutonium credit, $7 per gram; shipping cost, $5 per kilogram; thermal efficiency, 31.1 percent; interest on working capital, 10 percent; plant factor, 80 percent. Fabrication and reprocessing cost assumed to vary with throughputs of those facilities: for example, with nuclear industry of 15,000 megawatts (electrical) and fuel enriched to 2.656 percent, fabrication cost is $56.50 per kilogram and reprocessing is $38.00 per kilogram.

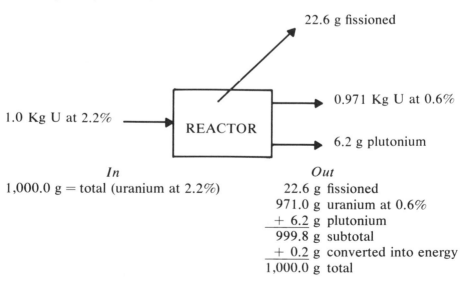

Figure 4–2. Illustrative mass balance around reactor

ORNL study, in the computer program we assume the coefficient to be a function of enrichment. The values of the P_X can easily be determined from a table published by the AEC. These values represent the AEC charges for enriched uranium. The most recent table is reproduced as table 4–3. We shall have more to say about the derivation of this table later.

Table 4–3. AEC uranium price schedule established 1 July 1962

Assay weight fraction	Base charge, dollars per kilogram U	Charge, dollars per gram of contained U-235
0.0005	3.00	6.00
0.0010	3.00	3.00
0.0020	3.00	1.50
0.0030	3.00	1.00
0.0040	3.70	0.93
0.0050	8.90	1.78
0.0060	15.35	2.56
0.0070	22.60	3.23
0.0080	30.50	3.82
0.0090	38.90	4.33
0.0100	47.70	4.77
0.015	95.30	6.35
0.020	146.50	7.33
0.030	254.30	8.48
0.040	365.80	9.15
0.050	479.40	9.59
0.10	1,062.00	10.62
0.50	5,882.00	11.76
0.90	10,808.00	12.01

Note: Cost of separative work = $30 per kilogram of uranium; cost of feed material = $23.50 per kilogram of uranium as UF_6; optimum tails composition = 0.0025307.
Source: E. A. Eschbach and M. F. Kanninen, *Uranium Price Schedules and Bred Fuel Value*, AEC Research and Development Report HW-72219, December 1964, p. 10.

The uranium is not in satisfactory condition to return to the AEC for credit immediately upon discharge from the reactor. First, the level of radiation must be allowed to decline. Notice that working capital cost is a function of this period. Second, the uranium must be chemically separated from the plutonium and fission products and converted into a form acceptable to the AEC. Nevertheless, accounting convention has well established the definition of consumption cost given in equation 4–1, and there is no advantage to be gained by challenging the convention. Logically, the credit for plutonium should also be included in the consumption cost expression, but it is normally treated as a separate element and will be so treated here.

The third main factor determining consumption cost is the cost of enrichment. In essence, this means that we must analyze the derivation of the AEC price list for enriched uranium, our table 4–3. The price list represents the total cost function of a production process with two inputs, natural uranium and separative work, and one output, enriched uranium.

Enrichment. The enrichment of uranium by the gaseous diffusion process was first accomplished during World War II at a plant built for weapons production. The first plant was built at Oak Ridge, Tennessee. Subsequently, similar plants were constructed at Paducah, Kentucky, and Portsmouth, Ohio. The fact that these plants are used to produce fissionable material for nuclear weapons has caused most of the data concerning production to be withheld from the public for national security reasons. Nevertheless, a considerable amount of public information is available and can be employed usefully for analysis.[4]

The principle of gaseous diffusion is that under the same driving pressure a gas of lower molecular weight will diffuse more quickly through a porous barrier than will a gas of higher molecular weight. The input to the plant is uranium hexafluoride, UF_6, in which the uranium proportion of the fissile isotope, uranium-235, is 0.711 percent (that percentage found in natural uranium). In one stage of the plant the uranium product may be enriched in uranium-235 by a factor of only 1.0043. Consequently, thousands of stages may be required to achieve a desired enrichment.

This large number of stages requires the large capital investment in gaseous diffusion plants, and the AEC investment in the three plants in the United States is $2,343,005,000.[5] The huge quantity of electric power required to drive the gas circulating pumps is illustrated by the power consumption figures given in table 4–4.

Leonard F. C. Reichle has published an attempt to estimate the capacity of the diffusion plants based entirely upon public information.[6] One measure of capacity is expressed in kilograms of separative work, which, as will be explained more fully later, are index units of the amounts of all plant inputs other than natural uranium feed. Reichle estimated the total capacity to be

4. In 1968 the AEC did declassify much technical and cost data in *AEC Gaseous Diffusion Plant Operations,* Report ORO-658, February, 1968. This report has rendered some of the analysis to follow obsolete.
5. U.S. Atomic Energy Commission, *1965 Financial Report* (Washington: Government Printing Office, 1965), p. 29.
6. "A Private Nuclear Power Economy," *Proceedings of the Atomic Industrial Forum, 1964,* 2 (December 1964): 96.

Table 4-4. Power consumption for three AEC gaseous diffusion plants (1965–1972 is forecast)

Year	Megawatts	Year	Megawatts
1950	400	1962	5,500
1951	425	1963	5,300
1952	700	1964	5,200
1953	1,000	1965	4,100
1954	2,000	1966	3,750
1955	3,900	1967	3,100
1956	6,300	1968	2,700
1957	6,550	1969	2,300
1958	6,000	1970	2,100
1959	6,000	1971	2,000
1960	6,000	1972	2,000
1961	6,000		

Source: U.S. Congress, Joint Committee on Atomic Energy, *AEC Authorizing Legislation Fiscal Year 1966, Part 1,* 89th Congress, 1st Session, January, February, and March 1965, p. 111. Figures were approximated from chart.

20.8 million kilograms of separative work.[7] He then transformed this estimate into the number of kilograms of 2.5 percent enriched uranium that could be produced, as shown in table 4–5.

In order to give some meaning to the capacity estimates, the demand side must be set forth. It is a complex problem in itself to forecast the growth rate of nuclear capacity, but since we are only interested in a rough quantitative comparison of demand with capacity, a high- and low-demand estimate is adequate. For this purpose we shall use predictions made by the AEC and published in March 1965. These nuclear capacity estimates are presented in table 4–6.

Based on the nuclear capacities in table 4–6, and by assuming fuel consumption characteristics of the reactors, the AEC has made estimates of the enriched uranium requirements of the free world. These estimates are presented in table 4–5. We have also computed the requirements for the United States alone, based on the AEC's statement that these requirements are approximately 47 percent of the total. The estimated capacities of the United States gaseous diffusion plants are also included in the table.

Whether the relevant demand for the AEC plants should be the requirements of the free world or the United States only is difficult to assess. The United States enriched uranium requirements are probably minimum ones,

7. The AEC report, *AEC Gaseous Diffusion Plant Operations,* Report ORO-658, February 1968, shows that Reichle overestimated capacity. The correct figure is 17.1 million kilograms of separative work.

Table 4–5. Estimated annual requirements for enriched uranium versus capacity of gaseous diffusion plants in the United States (in thousands of kilograms of uranium)

	Enriched uranium requirements				2.5 percent enriched uranium capacity in United States	
	Free world		United States			
Year	Low	High	Low	High	Amortization rate percentage	
					5.4	10.0
1967	300	400	141	188	6,350	7,900
1968	500	700	235	329		
1969	600	1,100	282	517		
1970	600	1,500	282	705		
1971	1,000	2,000	470	940		
1972	1,400	2,600	657	1,240		
1973	1,800	3,000	845	1,410		
1974	2,200	3,400	1,030	1,600		
1975	2,600	3,900	1,240	1,830		
1976	2,900	4,200	1,360	1,970		
1977	3,300	4,600	1,550	2,160		
1978	3,800	5,200	1,780	2,440		
1979	4,300	5,900	2,020	2,770		
1980	4,700	6,400	2,210	3,010		

Source: Estimated Growth of Civilian Nuclear Power, March 1965, p. 16. United States requirements were taken as 47 percent of free world requirements. Capacity estimates are based on figures given in Leonard F. C. Reichle, "A Private Nuclear Power Economy," *Proceedings of Atomic Industrial Forum, 1964,* 2 (December 1964): 96.

while some portion of foreign requirements may be captured. This of course will depend upon a number of factors which cannot be known now: the price of AEC enriched uranium relative to the price of British and French enriched uranium, the degree of necessity foreign countries may feel toward establishing domestic capability in enriching uranium, and the capacity of foreign enriching facilities.[8]

8. For example,
A $37.8 million modernization of the UK Atomic Energy Authority's diffusion plant will have the twofold objective of: (1) meeting the enriched uranium requirements of Britain's second generation nuclear power program without dependence on the U.S. and (2) enabling AEA to compete with U.S. AEC for European orders by the early-to-middle 1970s. (*Nucleonics,* 24 [February 1966]: 27).
Also, it was reported in *Nucleonics,* 23 (March 1965): 26, that the first stage of France's gaseous diffusion plant at Pierrelatte was dedicated in January 1965. Three further stages are scheduled to be in operation by the end of 1967. Unfortunately, capacity figures for these foreign plants are not public information, although at the present time they are certainly relatively small compared to United States plants.

Table 4–6. Cumulative installed nuclear capacity using enriched uranium (in thousands of megawatts)

Year	United States		Rest of free world	
	Low	High	Low	High
1965	1.9		0.5	
1966	2.3		1.1	
1967	3.6		1.1	
1968	4.6		2.1	
1969	4.8	5.3	2.4	
1970	6	7	5	6
1971	7	11	6	10
1972	9	16	8	15
1973	12	22	11	22
1974	16	29	16	29
1975	21	37	21	37
1976	27	46	27	46
1977	34	56	34	56
1978	42	67	42	67
1979	51	79	51	79
1980	61	92	61	92

Note: The Atomic Energy Commission has increased its United States nuclear capacity estimates. In 1969 the low and high estimates for 1980 were 130,000 and 170,000 megawatts, respectively (*The Nuclear Industry 1969*, p. 136).

Source: U.S. Atomic Energy Commission, *Estimated Growth of Civilian Nuclear Power*, Report TID-4500, March 1965, p. 14.

Another problem in delineating the relevant demand is the level of military requirements. The AEC's prediction of electric power consumption in diffusion plants for the next few years (table 4–4) would seem to imply that military requirements have been greatly curtailed. Also, an article in the *New York Times* in June 1964 states that net military requirements may possibly be considered as zero:

> The United States currently has a billion-dollar surplus of enriched uranium and a pending surplus of plutonium. In fact, even without the continuing production of the materials, the Atomic Energy Commission is reaching the point where the supply of the two materials recovered from obsolete weapons about equals requirements in the fabricating of new weapons.[9]

It must be recognized that the demand-capacity figures given in table 4–5 are dependent upon a number of important assumptions. Nevertheless, that

9. *New York Times*, 7 June 1964, sec. 1, p. 3.

57

AEC diffusion plants currently have and for some time into the future will continue to have considerable excess capacity is incontestable. This fact has given rise to a number of questions about the "correct" AEC pricing policy. We shall return to this problem after a rather intensive analysis of the production function of the gaseous diffusion plant.

Enrichment production function. The theory of isotope separation provides the structure for analyzing the production function of gaseous diffusion plants. An excellent presentation of the theory is contained in a nuclear chemical engineering text by Benedict and Pigford.[10] We shall briefly sketch the parts of this theory relevant to deriving the production function.

Figure 4–3 shows a schematic diagram of a diffusion plant and lists the symbols to be used. The two inputs are F, the feed, and S, the separative work. Of course the plant itself is a variable input in the long run, but for the

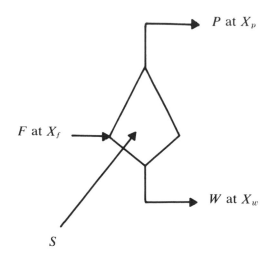

P at X_p

F at X_f

W at X_w

S

where P = kilograms of enriched uranium
X_p = weight fraction of U-235 in P
W = kilograms of waste, or tails
X_w = weight fraction of U-235 in W
F = kilograms of natural uranium
X_f = weight fraction of U-235 in F
S = kilograms of separative work

Figure 4–3. Schematic diagram of gaseous diffusion plant

10. Manson Benedict and Thomas H. Pigford, *Nuclear Chemical Engineering* (New York: McGraw-Hill, 1957), chap. 10.

moment we shall only be concerned with the short-run inputs. The output is P, the enriched uranium. The waste, W, is also an output of the plant, but as will be shown the fraction of uranium-235 in the waste, X_w, will be set at precisely that value which makes its economic value zero. At some time in the future, when the breeder reactors are nearing commercial applicability, the present value of the waste uranium as a breeder fuel will become positive,[11] but for the present analysis, this is ignored.

Consideration of figure 4–3 indicates that two material balance, or conservation equations for total uranium and for total uranium-235, can be written.

$$F = P + W. \tag{4-2}$$

$$FX_f = PX_p + WX_w. \tag{4-3}$$

The amount of product, P, is set equal to one kilogram (we are interested in the production function where output is the degree of enrichment of one unit of product, *not* where output is the number of units of a particular degree of enriched uranium). The assay, or weight fraction of uranium-235 in the natural uranium feed, X, is normally 0.00711. By substitution of equation 4–2 into equation 4–3, and rearranging terms, we get the expression:

$$X_p = F(X_f - X_w) + X_w. \tag{4-4}$$

Equation 4–4 describes all of the production possibilities. That is to say, for a given output, X_p, it is possible to produce that product assay by an infinite number of combinations of the amount of feed, F, and the waste assay, X_w. The common sense of the relation—the higher the waste assay, the more the required feed, and vice versa—is borne out by observing that the partial derivative of F with respect to X is always positive:

$$\frac{\partial F}{\partial X_w} = \frac{X_p - X_f}{(X_f - X_w)^2} > 0 \tag{4-5}$$

where $\qquad\qquad 1 > X_p > X_f > X_w > 0.$

But natural uranium feed is not the only short-run input. Every particular combination of F and X_w, for a given X_p, defines an associated amount of separative work input. For our purposes the separative work, S, can be viewed as a measure of the total flow required in a diffusion plant to achieve a given product enrichment.

The importance of the separative duty in isotope separation lies in the fact that it is a good measure of the magnitude of an isotope separation

11. Breeder reactors can use the depleted or waste uranium as the fertile material; plutonium as the fissile material will, upon fissioning, convert the waste (mostly uranium-238) into more fissile plutonium.

job. Many of the characteristics of the plant which make important contributions to its cost are proportional to the separative duty. For example, in a gaseous diffusion plant built as an ideal cascade of stages operated at the same conditions, the total flow rate, the total pump capacity, the total power demand, and the total barrier area are all proportional to the separative duty.[12]

The definitional equation for units of separative work is

$$S = V_p + FV_w - V_w - FV_f \qquad (4\text{--}6)$$

where
$$V_i = (2X_i - 1) \ ln \ \frac{X_i}{1 - X_i} \cdots i = p, w, f.$$

Since F in equation 4–6 is a function of X_p and X_w, it is clear that S is also a function of X_p and X_w. And further, for a given output and feed, S is a function of X_w alone. The common sense that the lower the waste assay the more the separative work, and vice versa, is borne out by differentiating S partially with respect to X_w.

$$\frac{\partial S}{\partial X_w} = (F - 1) \left[2 \ ln \left(\frac{X_w}{1 - X_w} \right) + \frac{2X_w - 1}{X_w(1 - X_w)} + \frac{V_w - V_f}{X_f - X_w} \right] < 0 \quad (4\text{--}7)$$

where
$$1 > X_p > X_f > X_w > 0.$$

In view of equations 4–5 and 4–7, for a given product, increasing the waste assay requires more F and less S, and decreasing X_w requires less F and more S. These relations are shown graphically in figure 4–4. By eliminating X_w between equations 4–4 and 4–6, it is possible, in principle, to derive a production function of the standard form,

$$X_p = f(F, S). \qquad (4\text{--}8)$$

Equation 4–8 can then be depicted in the conventional isoquant manner (see figure 2–8 of chapter 2).

Having set out the range of technical alternatives for producing X_p, it is

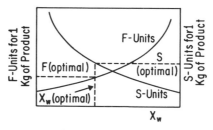

Figure 4–4. Determination of optimum allocation of inputs

12. Benedict and Pigford, p. 397.

now the function of the economics to determine the optimal economic choice. The fact that both inputs, F and S, are known functions of a single variable, X_w, enables the analytical selection of the optimal alternative to be rather simple. By expressing cost as a function of X_w it is possible to determine that value of X_w which minimizes cost. The known value of X_w may then be used to determine the optimal quantities of the two inputs. This procedure is illustrated graphically in figures 4–4 and 4–5: the waste assay which minimizes cost in figure 4–5 can be used in figure 4–4 to find the optimal amounts of F and S.

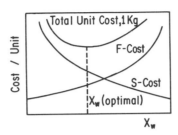

Figure 4–5. Determination of optimum waste composition

The problem has been formulated and solved analytically in Benedict and Pigford,[13] and we shall reproduce their method here. There is a fundamental difference, however, between our definition of the proper unit cost for separative work and the one in Benedict and Pigford.

$$C = P_f F + P_s S \qquad (4\text{–}9)$$

where
C = total unit cost of enriched uranium
F = units of feed
P_f = price of feed
S = units of separative work
P_s = price (unit cost) of separative work.

Substituting equations 4–4 and 4–6, after rearranging terms, into 4–9 gives:

$$C = \left[(V_p - V_f) - (X_p - X_f)\frac{V_f - V_w}{X_f - X_w}\right]P_s + \left(\frac{X_p - X_w}{X_f - X_w}\right)P_f. \qquad (4\text{–}10)$$

13. Ibid., p. 400.

The optimum waste assay, X_w, is that value which satisfies

$$\frac{dC}{dX_w} = 0 \qquad (4\text{--}11)$$

or

$$\frac{X_p - X_f}{X_f - X_w}\left(\frac{dV_w}{dX_w} - \frac{V_f - V_w}{X_f - X_w}\right)P_s + \frac{(X_p - X_f)}{(X_f - X_w)}\frac{P_f}{(X_f - X_w)} = 0 \qquad (4\text{--}12)$$

and

$$\left(\frac{dV_w}{dX_w} - \frac{V_f - V_w}{X_f - X_w}\right)P_s + \frac{P_f}{X_f - X_w} = 0. \qquad (4\text{--}13)$$

It is important to note that the last equation does not contain the term X_p, the product assay. This means that the optimal value of X_w is independent of the degree of enrichment of the product and depends only upon P_s and P_f.

Because of the difficulty of solving for X_w explicitly, iterative solutions for the optimum waste compositions have been performed. Table 4–7 gives some representative values as a function of the ratio of P_f to P_s. Thus, for any given ratio of P_f to P_s, the optimum waste assay can be selected and inserted into equation 4–10 to determine the minimum cost of product, X_p. This procedure, in fact, will generate the AEC Uranium Price Schedule shown in table 4–3 when P_f equals \$23.50 per kilogram and P_s equals \$30.00 per kilogram.

Table 4–7. Optimum tails composition

Ratio of feed cost to cost of separative work	Optimum tails composition, wt. percentage	Ratio of feed cost to cost of separative work	Optimum tails composition, wt. percentage
0.0	0.711	2.6	0.135
0.2	0.402	2.8	0.129
0.4	0.327	3.0	0.124
0.6	0.282		
0.8	0.250		
1.0	0.226		
1.2	0.207		
1.4	0.192		
1.6	0.179		
1.8	0.168		
2.0	0.158		
2.2	0.149		
2.4	0.142		

Source: Eschbach and Kanninen, p. 51.

As pointed out at the outset of this analysis, we have been concerned with a short-run production function. That is to say, we have considered the diffusion plants themselves as fixed and only considered the variable inputs in determining the optimum combination of inputs. Consequently, in our formulation P_s, the unit cost of separative work, should only include those cost elements which vary with changes in separative work requirements. Certainly capital charges of the diffusion plants are irrelevant in determining the optimal mix of feed and separative work. Capital charges are sunk costs and do not vary with the output of the plants.

Public information would seem to indicate that the AEC includes these irrelevant elements of cost in determining the optimum waste assay. Of course this is merely speculation on our part, but it seems worthwhile to elaborate on this point, whatever the actual production methods of the AEC may be.

An article by two members of the AEC Office of Operations Analysis and Planning published in January 1958 states that

> the major costs that are involved in producing material at some enrichment X_p are (a) the cost of the feed material and (b) the cost of separative work (plant-amortization and operating costs can both be included as part of the latter).[14]

The authors then proceeded to employ the two concepts of cost defined above in the same way that we used P_f and P_s. That is to say, P_s (including a portion for plant amortization) was used to derive the optimum tails assay for minimum cost. The same procedure was repeated in a more elaborate exposition in an official AEC publication by one of the authors.[15]

To illustrate the point, we shall make a calculation using the annual costs of the AEC gaseous diffusion plants as estimated by Reichle, who calculated that the total annual cost of the plants, operating at full capacity, is $624.6 million. It seems reasonable to assume that electricity consumption is the only cost element which is very sensitive to the amount of production taking place. Some of the other elements may have variable components, but we will regard them as essentially fixed costs, independent of the level of output. Since, in Reichle's estimate, total cost corresponds to a charge of $30 per kilogram of separative work, and the cost of electricity ($210 million) is roughly one-third of total cost, we shall select $10 per kilogram as our illustrative figure for the unit cost of the *variable* component of separative work.

Our procedure will be to calculate the reduction in cost of a kilogram of

14. Hal L. Hollister and Artha Jean Burington, "Pricing Enriched Uranium," *Nucleonics*, 16 (January 1958): 54.

15. U.S. Atomic Energy Commission, *Methods of Calculating U-235 Outputs and Charges by Use of Ideal Cascade Theory*, Report TID-8522, February 1960, p. 12.

2.5 percent enriched uranium if $10 per kilogram is used as P_s in lieu of $30 per kilogram. We shall assume the price used by the AEC for natural uranium, $23.50 per kilogram as UF_6 (corresponds to $8.00 per pound of U_3O_8). From table 4–7, the optimum tails composition when P_s is $30 per kilogram is 0.0025, and when $10 per kilogram is 0.0014.

The formula for the amount of natural uranium feed, F, can be derived from equation 4–4 for a product assay, X_p, of 2.5 percent.

$$F = \frac{0.025 - X_w}{0.0071 - X_w}. \tag{4–14}$$

The formula for the amount of separative work, S, is given by equation 4–6. Substituting the optimum tails assay, X_w, for each of the two separative work costs into equations 4–14 and 4–6 gives the results shown in table 4–8.

Table 4–8. Input amounts for one kilogram of 2.5 percent enriched uranium

	$P_s = \$30$	$P_s = \$10$
Feed, in kilograms	4.90	4.14
Separative work, in kilograms	2.83	3.79

Note: $P_f = \$23.50$ in both cases.

The amounts of feed and separative work agree with expectations. The higher the price of separative work relative to feed, the more separative

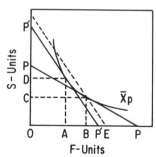

Figure 4–6. Resource cost of using incorrect price ratio of inputs in the production of enriched uranium

work will be curtailed. That is to say, feed will be substituted for separative work when the relative price of separative work is raised.

Figure 4–6 illustrates the issue. If we assume that the price (or unit cost) of S used by the AEC does include irrelevant capital charges, the AEC price ratio can be represented by the slope of PP. The correct price ratio (where P_s includes only cost elements which vary with the plant utilization rate) is given by the slope of $P'P'$. The hypothetical AEC solution calls for more feed (OB units versus OA units) and less separative work (OC units versus OD units) than economically optimal. The greater real cost of the AEC solution can be measured as $OE - OP'$ units of natural uranium feed.

To exemplify the rough order of magnitude of the assumed misallocation of resources, the saving per kilogram of product can be computed:

	Reduction in feed cost	Increase in separative work cost

Saving per kilogram $= (4.90 - 4.14)P_f - (3.79 - 2.83)P_s$

where

$P_f = \$23.50$ per kilogram
$P_s = \$10$ per kilogram,

or saving per kilogram $= \$8.30.$

If we take Reichle's estimate of capacity at 20.8 million kilograms of separative work as reasonable, the capacity in kilograms of 2.5 percent enriched uranium can be calculated by dividing that figure by the kilograms of separative work per kilogram of product, or 20.8 million/3.79, equals 5.5 million. The total annual saving for our example would then be approximately 5.5 million kilograms of product times $8.30 saving per kilogram, or $45.6 million.

It must be stressed that the preceding discussion has not made any mention of the AEC pricing policy, which will be discussed next. It is not suggested that the figure of $10 per kilogram be substituted for the $30 figure in generating the AEC price schedule. The $10 per kilogram figure is only relevant for determining the optimum mix of inputs: if the AEC policy is to recover capital cost, then this must be added to the variable cost.

Enrichment pricing policy. Discussion of the enriched uranium pricing problem of the AEC has often centered upon the recovery of capital charges. The reason for the interest in this aspect of pricing is due to the magnitude of the capital investment in diffusion plants and the low current and prospective plant utilization rates. Figure 4–7 illustrates the problem.

If the utilization rate is low, say OQ, then to enable the AEC to recover full cost the price must be set relatively high, at OP. Of course the greater

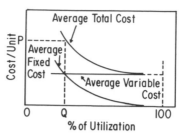

Figure 4–7. Short-run enrichment costs

the utilization rate, the lower the full cost recovery price. The AEC must reconcile two conflicting goals: a low price to encourage the nuclear industry and a high price to recover full cost.

In 1969 the AEC initiated toll enrichment services for privately owned natural uranium. The proposed criteria for these services were published in October 1965, and an excerpt is presented below to demonstrate the AEC pricing philosophy.

> AEC charges for enriching services will be established on a basis that will assure the recovery of appropriate Government cost projected over a reasonable period of time. The cost of separative work includes electric power and all other costs, direct and indirect, of operating the gaseous diffusion plants; appropriate depreciation of said plants; and a factor to cover applicable costs of process development, AEC administration and other Government support functions, and imputed interest on investment in plant and working capital. During the early period of growth of nuclear power, there will be only a small civilian demand on the large AEC diffusion plants. . . . In this interim period of low plant utilization, the Commission has determined that the costs to be charged to the separative work produced for civilian customers will exclude those portions of the costs attributable to depreciation and interest on plant investment which are properly allocable to plant in standby and to excess capacity.
>
> The contract shall specify for the term of the agreement a guaranteed ceiling charge, subject to upward escalation for the cost of electric power and labor. The ceiling charge as of July 1, 1965, the base date for application of escalation, is $30 per Kg unit of separative work for separation of U-235 from U-238.[16]

The quotation shows that the AEC, in trying to meet both goals (full cost recovery and a low price to stimulate the industry), has achieved a com-

16. *Federal Register,* 1 October 1965, p. 12551.

promise of sorts. Only full cost recovery of that portion of the plants actually in production is proposed.

Another reason for desiring a low price is to prevent potential competition in other countries from becoming actual. Unfortunately the determination of a sufficiently low price to prevent entry is more difficult than in the normal monopoly case. The thinking of other countries in regard to establishing enrichment facilities is influenced not only by economic motives but also by the complexity of national security pressures. Both Britain and France currently possess enrichment capability, and each will probably offer substantial competition to the United States in the future.

If the AEC should select economic efficiency as its goal in pricing enrichment services, the concern with recovering past investment could happily be discarded. Price should be equal to long-run marginal cost. Long-run marginal cost is concerned with future cost, including necessary investment, to provide enrichment services, not with historical World War II expenditures for huge diffusion plants for military purposes.

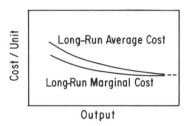

Figure 4–8. Long-run enrichment costs

Figure 4–8 is a likely example of the long-run cost function. Unfortunately, very little public information is available to suggest even the shape of the function, much less the values.[17] Economies of scale can be inferred from a statement made by an AEC official in January 1965:

> This means we have expanded by . . . [classified material deleted] the additional capacity which was the basis of the expansion design. This was accomplished for an investment of $200 million, whereas building from scratch a plant of this capacity would have involved an investment of about $750 million.[18]

17. As pointed out in note 4 above, the AEC did release cost data in 1968. These data indicate that figure 4–8 is roughly correct and that long-run marginal cost is around $21–23 per kilogram.

18. Statement of George F. Quinn in Joint Committee on Atomic Energy Hearings, *AEC Authorizing Legislation, Fiscal Year 1966, Part 1*, 89th Congress, 1st Session, January 1965, p. 80.

Table 4-9. Sensitivity of fuel cost to variation in price of natural uranium (in mills per kilowatt-hour)

Natural uranium (dollars per lb of U₃O₈)	Enrichment (percentage U-235)	Total	C	F	R	S	WC	P
4.00	2.57	1.28 (100)	.72 (56)	.29 (22)	.19 (15)	.03 (2)	.23 (18)	.17 (−13)
6.00	2.57	1.44 (100)	.85 (59)	.29 (20)	.19 (13)	.03 (2)	.26 (18)	.17 (−12)
8.00	2.55	1.59 (100)	.97 (61)	.29 (18)	.19 (12)	.03 (2)	.29 (18)	.17 (−10)
10.00	2.55	1.73 (100)	1.08 (62)	.29 (16)	.19 (11)	.03 (1)	.32 (19)	.17 (−10)
12.00	2.54	1.87 (100)	1.19 (63)	.29 (15)	.19 (10)	.03 (1)	.35 (19)	.17 (−9)
14.00	2.54	2.01 (100)	1.29 (64)	.29 (14)	.19 (9)	.03 (1)	.38 (19)	.17 (−8)
16.00	2.54	2.14 (100)	1.40 (65)	.29 (13)	.19 (9)	.03 (1)	.41 (19)	.17 (−8)

Note: Percentages are given in parentheses; C = consumption, F = fabrication, R = reprocessing, S = shipping, WC = working capital, P = plutonium credit.

Assumptions: Separative work cost, $30 per kilogram; plutonium credit, $7 per gram; shipping cost, $5 per kilogram; thermal efficiency, 31.1 percent; interest on working capital, 10 percent; plant factor, 80 percent. Fabrication and reprocessing cost assumed to vary with throughputs of those facilities: for example, with nuclear industry of 15,000 megawatts (electrical) and fuel enriched to 2.656 percent, fabrication cost is $56.50 per kilogram and reprocessing is $38.00 per kilogram.

Table 4-10. Sensitivity of fuel cost to variation in cost of separative work (in mills per kilowatt-hour)

Separative work (dollars per kilogram)	Enrichment (percentage U-235)	Total	C	F	R	S	WC	P
20.00	2.65	1.26 (100)	.70 (56)	.28 (22)	.18 (15)	.02 (2)	.23 (18)	.16 (-13)
22.00	2.65	1.30 (100)	.73 (57)	.28 (21)	.18 (14)	.02 (2)	.24 (18)	.16 (-12)
24.00	2.60	1.33 (100)	.76 (57)	.28 (21)	.19 (14)	.02 (2)	.24 (18)	.16 (-12)
26.00	2.60	1.37 (100)	.79 (58)	.28 (20)	.19 (14)	.02 (2)	.25 (18)	.16 (-12)
28.00	2.55	1.40 (100)	.82 (58)	.29 (20)	.19 (13)	.03 (2)	.25 (18)	.17 (-12)
30.00	2.55	1.44 (100)	.85 (59)	.29 (20)	.19 (13)	.03 (2)	.26 (18)	.17 (-12)

Note: Percentages given in parentheses; C = consumption, F = fabrication, R = reprocessing, S = shipping, WC = working capital, P = plutonium credit.

Assumptions: Natural uranium, $6.00 per pound of U_3O_8; plutonium credit, $7 per gram; shipping cost, $5 per kilogram; thermal efficiency, 31.1 percent; interest on working capital, 10 percent; plant factor, 80 percent. Fabrication and reprocessing cost assumed to vary with throughputs of those facilities: for example, with nuclear industry of 15,000 megawatts (electrical) and fuel enriched to 2.656 percent, fabrication cost is $56.50 per kilogram and reprocessing is $38.00 per kilogram.

Another possibility regarding future AEC policy toward the gaseous diffusion plants is the transfer of the plants to private control. Such a transfer would remove the government from the last major part of the fuel cycle.[19]

Tables 4–9 and 4–10 are presented to illustrate the effect of changing the price of uranium feed and separative work cost on total fuel cost. For each value of the parameter being varied, the costs are reported at that level of enrichment which minimizes total fuel cost. These two parameters can be seen to be quite significant: a change of 10 percent in the price of natural uranium is associated with a change of 3.5 percent in total fuel cost, and a change of 10 percent in the separative work cost is associated with a change of 3.6 percent in total fuel cost.

19. An article in the *New York Times,* November 16, 1969, reported that President Nixon had instructed the AEC to prepare its gaseous diffusion plants for sale. Several alternatives were suggested: (*a*) a government corporation like the Tennessee Valley Authority, (*b*) a completely private enterprise with companies buying one, two, or, less likely, all three AEC plants, (*c*) a joint venture between government and private industry, (*d*) a single agency like the American Telephone and Telegraph Company, and (*e*) a dual system with the AEC retaining its plants and private enterprise being allowed to build a new diffusion plant. Further materials on this subject are contained in U.S. Congress, Joint Committee on Atomic Energy, *Future Ownership of the AEC's Gaseous Diffusion Plants,* August 1969.

Chapter 5. Nuclear Fuel Cost: Other Components

The major component of the light water nuclear fuel cost, consumption, was analyzed in the preceding chapter. Here, we will analyze the remaining fuel cost components with the exception of natural uranium price. Chapter 6 will be concerned with natural uranium price determination.

Fabrication

The cost of fabricating enriched uranium into fuel elements is the second most important component of nuclear fuel cost. Fabrication presently involves converting UF_6 to UO_2, compacting the UO_2 into pellets, loading the pellets into cladding tubes, sealing the tubes, and assembling the tubes into bundles known as fuel elements. Given the assumptions made in table 4–2 of chapter 4, it accounts for roughly 20 percent of fuel cost.

In September 1964, General Electric released a price list for fuel fabrication.[1] The first core fuel fabrication price per kilogram for a 1,000-megawatt plant was listed as $102. Since the current (1966) nuclear capacity in the United States is very small, about 1,000 megawatts, the production function for fuel fabrication is quite different from what it is expected to be in the mid-seventies and eighties. Consequently, the cost of $102 is not appropriate for use in our benefit-cost analysis. The point is made in a statement by Dr. Baron of Burns and Roe, Incorporated, to a congressional hearing:

> Present costs are about a hundred dollars a kilogram. We can foresee by 1990, which is the period that we made our study, that this cost would reduce to $60 per kilogram. This is based again on a mass production operation. At the present time nuclear fuels essentially are a hand operation and costly from that standpoint. As we learn more about fabrication of fuels we will be able to standardize and this cost will come down.[2]

Fortunately, the Oak Ridge National Laboratory (ORNL) has made a

1. U.S. Congress, Joint Committee on Atomic Energy, *Nuclear Power Economics: Analysis and Comments, 1964*, October 1964, p. 50.
2. U.S. Congress, Joint Committee on Atomic Energy, *Development, Growth, and State of the Atomic Energy Industry*, April 1963, p. 668.

recent study of fuel fabrication costs for ten different plant capacities. That a different and more capital intensive production function is assumed than currently prevails is made clear by a quotation from that study.

> The reference plants are highly automated and accordingly yield a low ratio of operating to capital charges. As plant size is decreased, however, the advantages of automation become less. Finally, at low capacities a point is reached where the product is actually penalized by automation. In the case of such low production rates, the use of more operating personnel and fewer automatic features is advantageous. . . . The important consideration . . . is that costs at low capacities are extrapolations of data at higher production rates. Therefore, the costs at low capacities [nuclear capacity of less than about 7,400 megawatts], are probably somewhat high.[3]

Basically, the ORNL or Rosenthal report cost estimates for the ten plant capacities define an estimate of the long-run average cost function. A number of estimates were made for each plant capacity to illustrate the cost variations with different types of plants and loading methods. For our purposes, we have selected the estimates for the type of plant and loading method which had lowest costs. Specifically, the contact type of plant (in lieu of, say, remote type) which employs vibratory compaction will be the basis for our analysis.

Table 5–1 gives the ORNL cost estimates. Clearly, economies of scale are significant; however, as the quotation pointed out, costs at low capacities are probably somewhat high, thereby exaggerating the scale economies. The third column of the table shows the approximate amount of nuclear capacity which the corresponding fabrication plant could serve. For example, a single fabrication plant with a capacity of 1,300 metric tons per year could serve 37,000 megawatts of installed nuclear capacity. To place the 37,000 megawatts in perspective, the AEC has estimated that the United States will have between 27,000 and 46,000 megawatts of nuclear capacity in 1976 (see table 4–6 in chapter 4).

The long-run cost function given in table 5–1 was used to study the sensitivity of fuel cost to changes in fabrication cost. By ordinary least-squares techniques, the cost function was estimated to be:

$$F = e^{5.9571 - 0.3053 \ln T} \tag{5–1}$$

where F = fabrication cost in dollars per kilogram
T = fabrication plant throughput in metric tons per year.

A coefficient of determination of 0.978 was obtained. The results of the

3. Rosenthal report, p. 96.

Table 5–1. Long-run average fuel fabrication cost

Average cost (dollars per kilogram)	Fabrication plant capacity (metric tons per year)	Nuclear capacity[a] (megawatts)
114	130	3,700
71	260	7,410
64	345	9,830
61	394	11,200
58.5	448	12,800
56.5	510	14,500
52.5	669	19,100
47	1,073	30,600
45	1,300	37,000

[a]All fuel is assumed to be 2.5 percent enriched uranium. The relation between the capacity of the fabrication plant and the capacity of nuclear plants is given by:

$$\text{Fabrication capacity (metric tons per year)} = \frac{(\text{nuclear capacity})(\text{plant factor})(365)}{(\text{exposure})(\text{thermal efficiency})}$$

Source: Rosenthal report, pp. 101, 187.

analysis are given in table 5–2. It can be calculated that a change of 10 percent in fabrication cost is associated with a change of 2.2 percent in total fuel cost (when the fabrication cost function varies between 80 and 100 percent of the ORNL estimate).

The fact that the average cost function declines continuously over the range of outputs given in table 5–1 implies that marginal cost is always less than average cost. Marginal cost below average cost makes for an unstable market equilibrium if there is more than one firm: any firm can reduce its cost per unit by expanding output. That long-run marginal cost is always less than average cost can easily be shown analytically. Total cost, C, is simply the product of average cost, F, and throughput, T,

$$C = FT = Te^{5.9571 \ - \ 0.3053 \ ln \ T}, \tag{5–2}$$

and marginal cost, MC, is the derivative of total cost with respect to throughput,

$$MC = \frac{dC}{dT} = 0.6947 \ F. \tag{5–3}$$

This result has important implications for the future market structure in fuel fabrication. A strong economic pressure toward concentration should develop if the ORNL cost estimates are assumed to be valid. The price of fuel fabrication services in a concentrated industry should be expected to diverge from marginal cost more than in a less concentrated one.

The Joint Committee on Atomic Energy has been especially concerned

73

Table 5-2. Sensitivity of fuel cost to variation in fabrication cost (in mills per kilowatt-hour)

Fabrication[a]	Fuel cost	Enrichment (percentage U-235)	C	F	R	S	WC	P
0.80	1.37 (100)	2.50	.85 (62)	.23 (17)	.19 (14)	.03 (2)	.24 (18)	.17 (−12)
0.90	1.40 (100)	2.50	.85 (60)	.26 (19)	.19 (13)	.03 (2)	.25 (18)	.17 (−12)
1.00	1.44 (100)	2.55	.85 (59)	.29 (20)	.19 (13)	.03 (2)	.26 (18)	.17 (−11)
1.10	1.47 (100)	2.60	.85 (58)	.31 (21)	.19 (13)	.02 (2)	.27 (18)	.16 (−11)
1.20	1.51 (100)	2.60	.85 (56)	.34 (22)	.19 (12)	.02 (2)	.27 (18)	.16 (−11)

[a]Numbers in this column are factors, f, used to vary the average fabrication cost function:

$$F \text{ (dollars per kilogram)} = f(e^{5.9571 \, - \, 0.3053 \, \ln T}),$$

where T = fabrication plant throughput, in metric tons per year.

Note: Percentages given in parentheses. C = consumption, F = fabrication, R = reprocessing, S = shipping, WC = working capital, P = plutonium credit.

Assumptions: Natural uranium, $6 per pound of U_3O_8; separative work cost, $30 per kilogram; plutonium credit, $7 per gram; shipping cost, $5 per kilogram; thermal efficiency, 31.1 percent; interest on working capital, 10 percent; plant factor, 80 percent. Reprocessing costs assumed to vary with throughput of that facility: for example, with nuclear industry of 15,000 megawatts and fuel enriched to 2.656 percent, reprocessing cost is $38 per kilogram.

with this issue. Its concern, however, has been with the advantages reactor manufacturers have over independent fuel fabricators by virtue of having designed the fuel element initially and normally having a contract to supply the first few cores.

REPRESENTATIVE HOSMER. I think we have got our finger on a problem here, if we are going to have competition, how are we going to have competition unless you are talking about competition for the original design of the plant itself. The fellows who sell the first core sell the core for the life of the installation, unless, as an alternative to that, the utility companies make it part of the contract to get the design.[4]

The general response to this line of questioning by witnesses representing various sectors of the atomic industry was that the reactor manufacturers do have an advantage but that it is not overwhelming. For example, Kenneth Davis of the Bechtel Corporation said,

I really believe there is a sufficient flexibility in the design of any core and sufficient opportunity for reducing costs over the next few years so that a competition on the supplying of a new core for an existing reactor can be meaningful.[5]

There are at least two other factors relating to the future competitive situation in fuel fabrication which should be mentioned. Some concern for the small, independent fuel fabricator has been shown in regard to the financing of uranium inventory during fabrication. If the fabricator were required to meet this expense, there would be a greater barrier to entry for small firms. But as J. F. Young of General Electric has suggested, the "utility could encourage an independent supplier by consigning special nuclear materials."[6] The second factor is the effect of vertical integration of uranium production and fuel fabrication. Since there is only one partly integrated fuel fabricator at present,[7] it is a bit premature to assess this possibility.

There are some indications of the current degree of competition in fuel fabrication worth noting. In July 1964 *Nucleonics* reported the names of nineteen firms capable of supplying fuel fabrication services.[8] The August 1965 issue reported twenty-one firms: four were new firms while two of the July 1964 firms were omitted.[9]

In an industry as young as atomic energy, with technology changing rapidly, it is difficult to predict what the market structure will be in the future.

4. U.S. Congress, Joint Committee on Atomic Energy, *Private Ownership of Special Nuclear Materials, 1964,* June 1964, p. 70.
5. Ibid.
6. Ibid., p. 127.
7. Ibid., p. 164.
8. *Nucleonics,* 22 (July 1964): 62.
9. *Nucleonics,* 23 (August 1965): 202.

Nevertheless, if we regard the ORNL cost estimates as meaningful, a strong economic motive for firms to merge or withdraw from the industry should develop, and it appears probable that reactor manufacturers will become the main suppliers of fabrication services. In any event, we shall assume that an industry sufficiently competitive to allow cost to be a fair estimate of price will exist in the future.

Reprocessing

Reprocessing includes the cost of recovering unburned uranium and plutonium from irradiated fuel elements and disposing of fission products. Table 4–2 shows that the reprocessing cost is about 13 percent of fuel cost.

A commercial facility for reprocessing was completed in the last half of 1965. Previously, the AEC performed this function, guaranteeing the firm, Nuclear Fuel Services, a certain baseload of orders for its first five years as an inducement to enter the field.[10] The capacity of the plant is such that it can serve a maximum of less than a 5,000-megawatt nuclear power industry.[11] Since we are interested in a long-run cost function, it is important to get cost estimates for a number of plant capacities larger than the Nuclear Fuel Services plant. Fortunately, we can use the Rosenthal report for this purpose.

Before analyzing the results of that report, we should mention that General Electric is considering building a $15-million reprocessing plant which will compete with Nuclear Fuel Services. The General Electric plant would have a capacity of about 300 metric tons per year (equivalent to a nuclear capacity of about 8,500 megawatts) and could be in operation in 1970.[12]

Table 5–3 summarizes the cost estimates made by the ORNL for reprocessing. These costs can be interpreted as defining a long-run average cost function. The function was estimated by least squares to be

$$R = e^{8.2062 \, - \, 0.7323 \, \ln \, T} \tag{5-4}$$

where R = reprocessing cost in dollars per kilogram
  T = reprocessing plant throughput in metric tons per year.

A coefficient of determination of 0.999 was obtained.

Clearly, economies of scale are significant. Increasing returns are present throughout the range of capacities studied. The marginal cost function, MC,

10. U.S. Congress, Joint Committee on Atomic Energy, *Chemical Reprocessing Plant,* May 1963, p. 109.
11. Rosenthal report, p. 117.
12. *Power,* April 1965, p. 92.

Table 5-3. Long-run average reprocessing cost

Average cost (dollars per kilogram)	Reprocessing plant capacity (metric tons per year)	Nuclear capacity[a] (megawatts)
70–80	200	5,700
50.5	345	9,830
46	394	11,200
41.5	448	12,800
38	510	14,500
31.2	669	19,100
22	1,073	30,600

[a]All fuel is assumed to be 2.5 percent enriched uranium. The relation between the capacity of the fabrication plant and the capacity of the reprocessing plant is given by:

$$\text{Reprocessing capacity (metric tons per year)} = \frac{(\text{nuclear capacity})(\text{plant factor})(365)}{(\text{exposure})(\text{thermal efficiency})}.$$

Source: Rosenthal report, pp. 125, 187.

can be derived for reprocessing in the same way that it was done for fabrication. Hence,

$$MC = 0.2677 \ R. \tag{5-5}$$

The same conclusion that was reached for fabrication also holds for reprocessing: the large-scale economies should create an economic pressure toward a highly concentrated industry. The greater relative difference between marginal cost and average cost in reprocessing than in fabrication should make the pressure greater.

Table 5-4 gives the results of the computer analysis. It can be shown that a change of 10 percent in reprocessing cost is associated with a change of 0.9 percent in total fuel cost (when the reprocessing cost function varies between 80 and 100 percent of the ORNL estimate). By using the long-run cost function for fabrication and reprocessing, the computer program can be arranged to calculate the effect on fuel cost of increasing the nuclear capacity. That is to say, we assume that as nuclear power capacity grows there will always be available fabrication and reprocessing plants of optimal capacities to serve the power industry. This assumption would obviously hold only in an ideal world, but the results are interesting if only to indicate a floor to cost reduction (assuming a constant technology).

Table 5-5 gives these results. The decrement to fuel cost becomes progressively less as the nuclear industry expands. An increase in capacity from 8,000 to 12,000 megawatts permits a cost reduction of 0.11 mills per kilowatt-hour, while an increase in capacity from 28,000 to 32,000 mega-

Table 5-4. Sensitivity of fuel cost to variation in reprocessing cost (in mills per kilowatt-hour)

Reprocessing[a]	Fuel cost	Enrichment (percentage U-235)	C	F	R	S	WC	P
0.80	1.41 (100)	2.50	.85 (60)	.29 (21)	.15 (11)	.03 (2)	.26 (19)	.17 (−12)
0.90	1.42 (100)	2.55	.85 (59)	.29 (20)	.17 (12)	.03 (2)	.26 (19)	.17 (−12)
1.00	1.44 (100)	2.55	.85 (59)	.29 (20)	.19 (13)	.03 (2)	.26 (18)	.17 (−11)
1.10	1.45 (100)	2.55	.85 (58)	.29 (20)	.21 (14)	.03 (2)	.26 (18)	.17 (−11)
1.20	1.47 (100)	2.60	.85 (58)	.28 (19)	.22 (15)	.02 (2)	.25 (17)	.16 (−11)

[a]Numbers in this column are factors, f, used to vary the average reprocessing cost function:

$$R \text{ (dollars per kilogram)} = f(e^{8.2062 \ - \ .7323 \ ln \ T})$$

where T = reprocessing plant throughput, in metric tons per year.

Note: Percentages given in parentheses; C = consumption, F = fabrication, R = reprocessing, S = shipping, WC = working capital, P = plutonium credit.

Assumptions: Natural uranium, $6 per pound of U_3O_8; separative work cost, $30 per kilogram; plutonium credit, $5 per kilogram; thermal efficiency, 31.1 percent; interest on working capital, 10 percent; plant factor, 80 percent. Fabrication cost assumed to vary with throughputs of those facilities: for example, with nuclear industry of 15,000 megawatts and fuel enriched to 2.656 percent, fabrication cost is $56.50 per kilogram.

Table 5–5. Sensitivity of fuel cost to variation in capacity of nuclear power plants (in mills per kilowatt-hour)

Nuclear industry (megawatts)	Fuel cost	Enrichment (percentage U-235)	C	F	R	S	WC	P
8,000	1.60 (100)	2.70	.85 (53)	.33 (21)	.29 (18)	.02 (1)	.26 (16)	.16 (−10)
12,000	1.49 (100)	2.60	.85 (57)	.30 (20)	.22 (15)	.02 (2)	.26 (17)	.16 (−11)
16,000	1.43 (100)	2.55	.85 (59)	.28 (20)	.18 (12)	.03 (2)	.26 (18)	.17 (−12)
20,000	1.38 (100)	2.50	.85 (61)	.27 (19)	.15 (11)	.03 (2)	.26 (19)	.17 (−12)
24,000	1.35 (100)	2.45	.84 (63)	.26 (19)	.13 (10)	.03 (2)	.26 (19)	.17 (−13)
28,000	1.32 (100)	2.45	.84 (64)	.25 (19)	.12 (9)	.03 (2)	.26 (20)	.17 (−13)
32,000	1.30 (100)	2.45	.84 (65)	.24 (18)	.11 (8)	.03 (2)	.26 (20)	.17 (−13)

Note: Percentages given in parentheses; C = consumption, F = fabrication, R = reprocessing, S = shipping, WC = working capital, P = plutonium credit.

Assumptions: Natural uranium, $6 per pound of U_3O_8; separative work cost, $30 per kilogram; plutonium credit, $7 per gram; shipping cost, $5 per kilogram; thermal efficiency, 31.1 percent; interest on working capital, 10 percent; plant factor, 80 percent. Fabrication and reprocessing cost assumed to vary with throughputs of those facilities: for example, with nuclear industry of 15,000 megawatts and fuel enriched to 2.656 percent, fabrication cost is $56.50 per kilogram and reprocessing is $38 per kilogram.

watts permits a reduction of only 0.02 mills. This is due to the slopes of the cost curves becoming less steep and beginning to flatten out at the higher capacities.

The large total change in fuel cost with an increase in nuclear capacity over the range from 8,000 to 32,000 megawatts should be emphasized. The fuel cost could be reduced from 1.60 to 1.30 mills per kilowatt-hour, or by 10 percent, simply through the exploitation of economies of scale. The AEC has estimated that nuclear capacity will be 7,000–11,000 megawatts in 1971 and 21,000–37,000 megawatts in 1975.

The assumption that minimum-cost plants, designed exclusively for the water reactors, serve the entire industry in fabrication and reprocessing does not necessarily exaggerate cost reduction. Of the factors abstracted from by this assumption, two would tend to decrease the cost reduction, and another would tend to increase the reduction. Undoubtedly there will be more than a single firm in each industry; since a single firm would have lowest cost, this factor tends to increase cost. One would generally expect that the smaller the number of firms, the greater their price-setting power. Thus cost reducing effects of greater volume may not be passed on to customers. As an offsetting factor, cost-cutting technological change will surely take place.

Shipping

The shipping cost includes the cost of fuel shipments from the fabrication plant to the reactor, and from the reactor to the reprocessing plant. Table 4–2 shows that shipping cost is relatively minor, accounting for only about 2 percent of fuel cost. For this reason, we will omit further study of it. A figure of $5 per kilogram, an average of the figures estimated by the ORNL in the Rosenthal report, will be used throughout our study for shipping cost.[13]

Working Capital

As explained in chapter 1, working capital cost could logically be considered as a component of either fuel cost or capital cost. Since it depends upon a number of parameters of the fuel cycle, we will class it as a fuel cost. Table 4–2 shows that the working capital cost is about 18 percent of fuel cost.

The working capital required for a nuclear plant is significantly greater than for a fossil fuel plant. One power company has stated that the working

13. Rosenthal report, p. 187.

capital requirement for a nuclear plant is \$22–\$30 per kilowatt compared to only \$3–\$4 per kilowatt for a fossil fuel plant.[14] There are two principal determinants of this cost: the amount of working capital and the interest rate. We shall consider the amount of working capital required first.

The fact that outlays for various components of fuel cost must precede the revenues derived from the fuel gives rise to the need for working capital. For example, a power company must pay for both the enriched uranium and the fuel fabrication services before the fuel element can even be shipped to the reactor site. At the reactor site the fuel is transformed into the electricity from which the company derives its revenues.

The actual requirement for working capital will vary from plant to plant. It will depend upon the financial arrangements made by each particular firm. More basically, it will depend upon certain key parameters of the fuel cycle, e.g., cost of enriched uranium, fabrication cost, irradiation period, reprocessing cost, and credits for recovered uranium and plutonium. For our purposes, we will make use of a formula derived by John M. Vallance of the AEC to approximate the amount of working capital.[15]

$$\text{Amount} = 0.75A + \frac{t}{2}(A + B) + 0.75B \qquad (5\text{--}6)$$

$$A = U_i + F, \text{ in dollars per kilogram of uranium}$$

$$B = U_f + P - R, \text{ in dollars per kilogram of uranium}$$

where
t = residence time of fuel in reactor in years
U_i = feed enriched uranium cost
F = fabrication cost
U_f = discharge enriched uranium cost
P = plutonium credit
R = reprocessing cost.

The coefficients of the A and B in the formula are approximations of the "effective" years for which those expenditures require working capital. Working capital cost, in dollars per kilogram is simply

$$WC = i[0.75A + \frac{t}{2}(A + B) + 0.75B], \qquad (5\text{--}7)$$

where
WC = working capital cost
i = interest rate.

14. Jersey Central Power and Light Company, *Report on Economic Analysis for Oyster Creek Nuclear Electric Generating Station*, p. 8.
15. John M. Vallance, "Fuel Cycle Economics of Uranium Fueled Thermal Reactors," paper given at the Third United Nations International Conference on the Peaceful Uses of Atomic Energy, May 1964, p. 5.

The appropriate interest rate has been the subject of some discussion. During the early years, when most power systems will have only one or two nuclear plants, it has been suggested that the near-cyclical part of working capital could be financed by short-term bank loans.[16] This rate is presumed to be less than the normal return required by power companies to finance fixed capital. Since we are interested in a period when power systems should have a number of nuclear plants, this financial device is not relevant. A study by the Atomic Industrial Forum concludes that "the cost of financing such inventories will rise in the long run . . . to a level of the composite cost of money to the reactor operator."[17]

The composite cost of money to a power company will vary from firm to firm according to difference in firms' prospective earnings and state and local taxes. The inclusion of taxes in an economic study depends upon the purpose of the study. We will include them because they affect the investment decisions of firms, which in turn affect the rate of growth of nuclear capacity. In the calculation of the economic benefits of the advanced converter development program, taxes should be excluded since they do not reflect true resource costs. However, since benefits are defined as the cost difference between light water and advanced reactors, taxes effectively cancel.

The Rosenthal report used a rate of 10 percent,[18] which consists roughly of a "return on money invested" of 6 percent (equivalent to financing with one-third capital returning 9 percent after taxes and two-thirds debt capital at 4.5 percent interest) and federal, state, and local taxes of about 4 percent.[19] The Jersey Central Power and Light Company used a rate of 10.39 percent in the economic analysis of the Oyster Creek nuclear plant.[20] In our computer analysis we shall vary the rate over the range from 6 percent to 24 percent and use 10 percent as a reference rate.

Table 5–6 gives the results of the analysis. A change of 10 percent in the interest rate will change the fuel cost by 1.6 percent (when the interest rate varies between 7 and 10 percent). Notice that when the interest rate is 10 percent, a change of 10 percent is equivalent to a change of one percentage point. Thus increasing the interest rate from 10 to 11 percent will increase fuel cost by 1.6 percent.

16. L. Geller et al., "Analyzing Power Costs for Nuclear Plants, "*Nucleonics,* 22 (July 1964): 67.

17. "Financing Privately Owned Nuclear Fuel Inventories," Report of the Ad Hoc Committee on Financing Nuclear Fuels, February 1963, p. 7.

18. Rosenthal report, p. 9.

19. Ibid., p. 215.

20. *Report on Economic Analysis for Oyster Creek Nuclear Electric Generating Station,* p. 10.

Table 5–6. Sensitivity of fuel cost to variation in working capital interest rate (in mills per kilowatt-hour)

Working capital interest rate (percentage)	Fuel cost	Enrichment (percentage U-235)	C	F	R	S	WC	P
6	1.33 (100)	2.65	.85 (64)	.28 (21)	.18 (14)	.02 (2)	.16 (12)	.16 (−12)
8	1.39 (100)	2.60	.85 (61)	.28 (20)	.19 (13)	.02 (2)	.21 (15)	.16 (−12)
10	1.44 (100)	2.55	.85 (59)	.29 (20)	.19 (13)	.03 (2)	.26 (18)	.17 (−11)
12	1.49 (100)	2.50	.85 (57)	.29 (20)	.19 (13)	.03 (2)	.31 (21)	.17 (−11)
16	1.59 (100)	2.45	.84 (53)	.30 (19)	.19 (12)	.03 (2)	.41 (26)	.17 (−11)
20	1.69 (100)	2.40	.84 (50)	.30 (18)	.19 (11)	.03 (2)	.50 (30)	.18 (−10)
24	1.80 (100)	2.40	.84 (47)	.30 (17)	.19 (11)	.03 (2)	.61 (34)	.18 (−10)

Note: Percentages given in parentheses: C = consumption, F = fabrication, R = reprocessing, S = shipping, WC = working capital, P = plutonium credit.

Assumptions: Natural uranium, $6 per pound of U_3O_8; separative work cost, $30 per kilogram; plutonium credit, $7 per gram; shipping cost, $5 per kilogram; thermal efficiency, 31.1 percent; plant factor, 80 percent. Fabrication and reprocessing cost assured to vary with throughputs of those facilities: for example, with nuclear industry of 15,000 megawatts and fuel enriched to 2.656 percent, fabrication cost is $56.50 per kilogram and reprocessing is $38 per kilogram.

Plutonium

The AEC currently will buy plutonium produced in reactors for a price of $10 per gram.[21] The 1964 Private Fuels Ownership Law requires that this guaranteed "buy-back" end by 1 January 1971. Since the plutonium credit accounts for approximately 10–15 percent of fuel cost, we must examine plutonium price determination in the period after 1970.

Plutonium is a heavy, radioactive, highly toxic element. It is a man-made element first identified in experiments conducted by Seaborg, Kennedy, McMillan, and Wahl at the University of California in 1940.[22] The principal isotope is plutonium-239, which is one of the three primary fissionable materials. Plutonium is an extremely hazardous material because of its radioactivity, and semiremote handling techniques must be used. An important advantage plutonium has over uranium-235 is that plutonium is chemically separable from uranium-238, while uranium-235 is not. The high cost of enrichment operations dictates that some uranium-235 be left in depleted uranium tails, whereas all plutonium can be extracted. A disadvantage of plutonium results from its toxicity. Since plutonium requires special handling, higher costs for fuel element fabrication and jacketing can be expected.

The AEC credit for plutonium through June 1962 ranged between $30 and $45 per gram, depending upon the grade (amount of undesirable isotopes present). From June 1962 through June 1963 the credit was $30 per gram, regardless of the grade.[23] The current AEC credit, $10 per gram, is based upon extensive studies of the thermal value of plutonium relative to that of uranium-235. Since the technology for burning plutonium will probably not be available until 1975, the current market valuation of plutonium would be less than $10 per gram.

There appear to be three distinct periods we should discuss: 1971–1974, 1975–1984, and 1985 and after.

1971–1974. In the first period, the primary demand for plutonium will be for research and development programs. Milton Shaw, director of the AEC reactor development division, has stated that "collective plutonium needs will exceed available supply from power reactors until about the mid-1970's."[24] In a study published in June 1965[25] an Edison Electric Institute committee made forecasts of the quantities of plutonium produced and required for this period. Their figures for the years 1971–1974 are given in table 5–7. The requirements figures represent only those research and development programs known at the time of preparation of the report.

---

21. The plutonium must be the product of fuel material leased or purchased from the AEC.
22. John F. Hogerton, *The Atomic Energy Deskbook* (New York: Reinhold, 1963), p. 402.
23. Ibid., p. 364.
24. *Nucleonics,* 24 (April 1966): 18.
25. Edison Electric Institute, *Plutonium Survey, 1964,* prepared by the EEI Committee on Nuclear Fuels, New York, June 1965. Referred to hereafter as *Plutonium Survey.*

Table 5-7. Estimated plutonium production and requirements

Calendar year	Known requirements of plutonium for research and development programs (kllograms)	Plutonium recovery (kilograms)
1971	2,330	1,520
1972	2,915	1,900
1973	1,950	2,080
1974	400	3,200

Source: Edison Electric Institute, *Plutonium Survey, 1964,* prepared by the EEI Committee on Nuclear Fuels, New York, June 1965, pp. 6, 16.

Perhaps the figures should therefore be viewed as a floor to requirements. The recovery figures are also quite uncertain. For example, a recent estimate places 1974 recovery at 6,377 kilograms, or almost double the EEI prediction.[26]

We have defined the periods of analysis by the years 1975 and 1985 because (a) recycle of plutonium in thermal, or light water, reactors is generally expected to become economic in 1975, and (b) fast breeder reactors fueled with plutonium are generally expected to become economic in 1985. Changes in these dates may well occur as time passes.

1975–1984. Plutonium recycle can be accomplished in various fuel cycle arrangements: (a) by enriching natural uranium with plutonium produced in the previous irradiation period, (b) by using plutonium with slightly enriched uranium, or (c) by recycling the plutonium in a reactor type other than that in which it is produced.[27]

If we assume that the recycle of plutonium will indeed become available in 1975, the plutonium credit for management purposes at that time should be reckoned at what is generally termed plutonium value, which is "the price that yields the same fuel cost whether a reactor is fueled with plutonium or with uranium."[28] Most plutonium value studies have been performed at the AEC Pacific Northwest Laboratory.[29]

26. *Nucleonics,* 24 (April 1966): 17.
27. E. A. Eschbach and S. Goldsmith, "Using Plutonium in Thermal Reactors," *Nucleonics,* 21 (January 1963): 49.
28. Ibid., p. 50.
29. The complexity of the studies is due to the fact that each type of reactor uses fuel somewhat differently, thereby giving varying plutonium values. Some of the reports describing the studies are: E. A. Eschbach, *A Survey of the Economics of Plutonium as a Fuel in Thermal Reactors,* AEC Research and Development Report HW-75338, 1962; Eschbach, "Plutonium Value Analysis," in *Proceedings of the Third United Nations International Conference on the Peaceful Uses of Atomic Energy,* vol. 11, New York, 1965; Eschbach, "Utilization of Plutonium in Fast and Thermal Reactors," 1963; and Eschbach and Kanninen, *Uranium Price Schedules and Bred Fuel Value,* AEC Research and Development Report HW-72219, December 1964.

We will assume that each reactor operator in this period recycles plutonium produced earlier in his own reactors. Plutonium recycling can be viewed as a technological advance in the use of uranium. Uranium requirements will simply be reduced. For example, based on AEC assumptions given in the next chapter, estimated annual uranium requirements in 1980 can be reduced by about one-third. Perhaps a more fruitful approach would be to consider the market for "total" uranium in which the supply function would be the sum of the individual uranium and plutonium (plutonium expressed in uranium equivalents) supply functions. Knowing the market price for uranium would then permit plutonium value to be calculated.[30] Production theory makes the point clear. For a firm to achieve least cost, the following condition must hold (for a continuous and differentiable production function):

$$\partial Q/\partial U \Big/ P_u = \partial Q/\partial P \Big/ P_p \qquad (5\text{--}8)$$

where
Q = output units
U = uranium units
P = plutonium units
P_u = uranium price
P_p = plutonium value.

Equation 5–8 specifies that the marginal product obtained for the last dollar expended on uranium must equate to the marginal product of the last dollar expended on plutonium. A better arrangement of the equation is

$$P_p = P_u \left(\frac{\partial Q/\partial P}{\partial Q/\partial U} \right). \qquad (5\text{--}9)$$

Equation 5–9 shows that plutonium value is directly proportional to the price of uranium. The factor of proportionality is the ratio of the marginal products of plutonium and uranium.

1985 and after.   The introduction of fast breeders in 1985 will have an important effect upon the relative prices of uranium and plutonium. Table 2–1 in chapter 2 shows that the number of neutrons emitted per neutron absorbed in fuel is about the same for plutonium and uranium-235 in thermal reactors. In fast reactors, however, the number of neutrons emitted by plutonium is significantly higher than by uranium-235; viz., 2.74 versus 2.18. This nuclear property makes plutonium a much better potential breeder fuel than uranium-235. In other words, the ratio of the marginal product of plu-

---

30. In chapter 6, in which uranium price determination is analyzed, we follow the first procedure. That is to say, we subtract plutonium from demand rather than adding it to supply.

tonium to that of uranium will be higher in breeders than it is in light water reactors.

Equation 5–9 can clearly show the change in relative prices of plutonium and uranium. The factor in parentheses will increase when fast breeders are introduced, thereby increasing plutonium value relative to uranium price. Within the range of nuclear growth predictions and assumptions used in the next chapter, the requirements for plutonium for fast breeders exceed the supply until well into the next century. As long as this condition holds, and other uses for plutonium do not materialize, it is reasonable to expect the market price of plutonium to tend toward plutonium value. An Edison Electric Institute committee has estimated that plutonium price will increase by as much as 50 percent by its use in fast breeders.[31]

Looking past the turn of the century, we can envisage a time when plutonium breeders can supply all plutonium requirements for nuclear capacity additions. This point in time can be defined as that point when breeder "doubling-time" becomes equal to or less than the "doubling-time" of nuclear power capacity.[32] Excess plutonium can then be used to fuel thermal reactors, with a probable decline in price.

Price prediction. Obviously, we cannot predict plutonium prices without considering uranium prices simultaneously, but the next chapter analyzes uranium, and we will base our plutonium price prediction upon those results.

Although the guaranteed buy-back price is terminated by law at the end of 1970, most of the plutonium demand for research and development in the 1971–1974 period will be by the AEC. Since we expect uranium to be about $6 per pound in 1975, we will select $9 per gram for the price of plutonium in 1975 (this is the estimated thermal value with uranium at $6 per pound).[33] This estimate agrees well with the Edison Electric Institute report, which stated that "if the use of plutonium as thermal reactor fuels is developed sufficiently during the next six years, the market price of plutonium is expected to hold close to the present price of $10 per gram . . . during the 1970s."[34] Jersey Central Power and Light Company has estimated that the

31. *Plutonium Survey,* p. 3. Also, some Atomic International analysts have estimated plutonium value in a breeder economy to range from about $13 to $22 per gram, based upon a natural uranium price of $6 per pound of U_3O_8. The corresponding plutonium value prior to breeder introduction ranges from about $7 to $11 per gram (D. J. Stoker, S. Golan, and S. Siegel, "Wanted: A Balanced Nuclear Economy," *Nucleonics,* 21 [June 1963]: 80).

32. Breeder "doubling-time" is the time required for a breeder to produce a net amount of plutonium equal to its core inventory. A ten-year breeder doubling-time is probably a reasonable estimate. Nuclear capacity doubling-time will be much shorter in the early years.

33. John M. Vallance, "Economics of the Conversion of Nuclear Energy to Electricity," *Proceedings of the American Chemical Society,* Detroit, April 1965, p. 81.

34. *Plutonium Survey,* p. 3.

Table 5–8. Sensitivity of fuel cost to variation in plutonium credit (in mills per kilowatt-hour)

Plutonium (dollars per gram)	Fuel cost	Enrichment (percentage U-235)	C	F	R	S	WC	P
3.00	1.51 (100)	2.65	.85 (56)	.28 (18)	.18 (12)	.02 (2)	.25 (16)	.07 (−5)
5.00	1.48 (100)	2.60	.85 (58)	.28 (19)	.19 (13)	.02 (2)	.25 (17)	.12 (−8)
7.00	1.44 (100)	2.55	.85 (59)	.29 (20)	.19 (13)	.03 (2)	.26 (18)	.17 (−11)
9.00	1.40 (100)	2.50	.85 (60)	.29 (21)	.19 (13)	.03 (2)	.27 (19)	.22 (−15)
11.00	1.36 (100)	2.45	.84 (62)	.30 (22)	.19 (14)	.03 (2)	.27 (20)	.27 (−20)
13.00	1.32 (100)	2.40	.84 (64)	.30 (23)	.19 (14)	.03 (2)	.28 (21)	.33 (−25)

Note: Percentages given in parentheses; C = consumption, F = fabrication, R = reprocessing, S = shipping, WC = working capital, P = plutonium credit.

Assumptions: Natural uranium, $6 per pound of U_3O_8; separative work cost, $30 per kilogram; shipping cost, $5 per kilogram; thermal efficiency, 31.1 percent; interest on working capital, 10 percent; plant factor, 80 percent. Fabrication and reprocessing cost assumed to vary with throughputs of those facilities: for example, with nuclear industry of 15,000 megawatts and fuel enriched to 2.656 percent, fabrication cost is $56.50 per kilogram and reprocessing is $38 per kilogram.

price will be $8 per gram in this period.[35] We shall select $7 per gram in the early 1970s, following the Rosenthal report.

In anticipation of 1985 and the greater productivity of plutonium in fast breeders, and a higher price, plutonium producers may gradually tend to stock, rather than recycle, plutonium. The Edison Electric Institute committee concludes: "During the late 1970s and early 1980s, the development of fast reactors and optimum plutonium use in thermal reactors are expected to increase the market price of plutonium, possibly to as much as $15 per gram."[36] For a somewhat more conservative estimate, we shall select a figure of $13 per gram for 1985.

The results of our sensitivity analysis of fuel cost with respect to changes in the plutonium credit are given in table 5–8. A change of 10 percent in the plutonium credit can be shown to cause a change of 1.1 percent in fuel cost (when plutonium credit ranges from $7 to $9 per gram).

Exposure

Exposure refers to the quantity of heat released from a unit of fuel during irradiation. As was explained earlier in this chapter, a positive relation between fuel enrichment and exposure has been assumed for the computer program. The specific relation was estimated from physics data reported in the Rosenthal report.[37]

Since only 1 or 2 percent of the fuel can be fissioned during one irradiation period, the natural approach in attempting to increase exposure (for constant enrichment) is to examine the reasons for this low utilitization rate. That is to say, given exposure as a unique function of enrichment, what are the limits which prevent the function from shifting upward?

There are two restraints on the exposure function: the loss of reactivity and mechanical failure.[38]

Loss of nuclear reactivity is due to the consumption of fissionable atoms and the accumulation of neutron-absorbing fission products. Mechanical failure may be caused by structural failure of the fuel which impedes coolant flow, or by the failure of fuel cladding, permitting release of fission products into the coolant flow, or by the failure of fuel cladding, permitting release of fission products into the coolant to such an extent

35. *Report on Economic Analysis for Oyster Creek Nuclear Electric Generating Station,* p. 24.
36. *Plutonium Survey,* p. 2.
37. Rosenthal report, pp. 153–154.
38. An excellent discussion of these phenomena is contained in the Edison Electric Institute report, *Survey of Initial Fuel Costs of Large U.S. Nuclear Power Stations,* December 1958, p. 11.

that the reactor has to be shut down for removal of defective fuel pieces.[39]

The exposure function can therefore be shifted upward by techniques which raise the lower of the two limits. For example, "major increases in burnup may be achieved by rearranging the fuel one or more times before it is discharged or by using several enrichment zones in order to extend the reactivity lifetime of the fuel."[40] Also, "another method for extending the reactivity limit . . . is to replace fuel very frequently in small batches."[41]

The important point for the economics is that considerable uncertainty is present in specifying an exposure function. The technology is at an early stage; hence it seems plausible to anticipate developments which will permit significant increases in exposure. That the payoff to such developments is so great should assure this result. Table 5–9 illustrates the sensitivity of fuel cost to changes in the exposure function. An increase of 10 percent in exposure can cause a reduction of 8.5 percent in fuel cost (when exposure varies between 80 and 100 percent of the exposure function assumed in the computer program).

Thermal Efficiency

Thermal efficiency is the percentage of total heat released in the nuclear reactor which is transformed into electrical energy. This efficiency depends upon the design and performance of the entire power station; it is closely related to the levels of operating temperature and pressure.

Some representative design thermal efficiencies for recent light water nuclear plants are shown in table 5–10. Thermal efficiencies in nuclear plants are much lower than in fossil fuel plants (efficiencies in modern fossil fuel plants range from 38 to 41 percent). Nuclear plants must operate at lower temperatures and pressures because of the physical characteristics of the coolant and materials of construction. On the other hand, because nuclear fuel costs are relatively low, the payoff to improved steam conditions is less than for, say, conventional plants in high-cost fossil fuel areas.

An AEC program to develop nuclear superheat may significantly alter this situation. For example, the AEC director of reactor development has testified that nuclear superheat may permit the thermal efficiency of boiling water plants to be increased to about 38 percent.[42] The total AEC investment in the program through March 1965 was about $16–$18 million, and the program terminated in December 1966.[43] An economic analysis of this

39. Ibid.
40. Ibid., p. 14.
41. Ibid., p. 16.
42. *AEC Authorizing Legislation, Fiscal Year 1966, Part 3*, p. 1301.
43. Ibid.

90

Table 5-9. Sensitivity of fuel cost to variation in exposure (in mills per kilowatt-hour)

Exposure[a]	Fuel cost	Enrichment (percentage U-235)	C	F	R	S	WC	P
0.80	1.74 (100)	2.50	1.06 (61)	.34 (20)	.20 (11)	.03 (2)	.32 (19)	.21 (−12)
0.90	1.57 (100)	2.55	.94 (60)	.31 (20)	.19 (12)	.03 (2)	.29 (18)	.18 (−12)
1.00	1.44 (100)	2.55	.85 (59)	.29 (20)	.19 (13)	.03 (2)	.26 (18)	.17 (−11)
1.10	1.33 (100)	2.55	.77 (58)	.27 (20)	.18 (14)	.02 (2)	.24 (18)	.15 (−11)
1.20	1.23 (100)	2.55	.70 (57)	.26 (21)	.18 (15)	.02 (2)	.21 (17)	.14 (−11)

[a] Numbers in this column are factors, f, used to vary the exposure function:

$$X(\text{megawatt} - \text{days per kg}) = f(161.75 + 36.8 \ln I)$$

where I = enrichment of fuel.

Note: Percentages given in parentheses; C = consumption, F = fabrication, R = reprocessing, S = shipping, WC = working capital, P = plutonium credit.

Assumptions: Natural uranium, $6 per pound of U_3O_8; separative work cost, $30 per kilogram; plutonium credit, $7 per gram; shipping cost, $5 per kilogram; thermal efficiency, 31.1 percent; interest on working capital, 10 percent; plant factor, 80 percent. Fabrication and reprocessing cost assumed to vary with throughputs of those facilities: for example, with nuclear industry of 15,000 megawatts and fuel enriched to 2.656 percent, fabrication cost is $56.50 per kilogram and reprocessing is $38 per kilogram.

Table 5–10. Representative design thermal efficiencies for recent light water nuclear plants

Plant	Megawatts	Thermal efficiency (percentage)
San Onofre	429	33.4
Connecticut Yankee	462	31.4
Oyster Creek	515	32.2
Dresden-2	715	31.0

Source: Electrical World, 14 June 1965, pp. 97–98.

program is needed and should be integrated with such an analysis of the advanced converter development program. Unfortunately, because of the scope of our study, we cannot pursue this problem here.

A reactor manufacturer has made some striking estimates of the cost reductions attendant upon successful implementation of nuclear superheat. At this point, of course, we are concerned mainly with the effect upon thermal efficiency, but it is necessary to consider related capital cost reductions also.

> The capital cost of the plant is less for the superheat reactor, particularly in the conventional portion of the plant. . . . In the conventional portion of the plant, most of these cost savings result from the reduced steam flow of the superheat steam cycle. Thus, the costs of the turbine, condenser, . . . are reduced. . . . Allis-Chalmers studies indicate that savings in capital costs for conventional equipment will be in the range of $6 to $8 per kilowatt, depending upon the steam conditions selected. . . . [C]ost savings within the nuclear steam generator of up to $2 per kilowatt are forecast.
>
> The improved net plant efficiency for the superheat reactor (35 to 37 percent for the next several plants) over the saturated boiling water reactor (32 to 33 percent) results in . . . a lower fuel consumption rate. For the moment, these reductions in fuel consumption are not directly reflected in the fuel cycle costs because of the higher fuel enrichments required in superheat reactor. . . . We believe that advances in superheat technology will bring about decreases in the required fuel enrichments, approaching those of the saturated boiling water reactor.
>
> We estimate that integral superheat reactors of the near future will produce electrical power at a 3-to-6 percent cost saving over the saturated boiling water reactor.[44]

44. Letter from H. C. Nickel, general manager, Atomic Energy Division of Allis-Chalmers, to Representative Holifield, dated 13 August 1965, reprinted in U.S. Congress, Joint Committee on Atomic Energy, *Development, Growth, and State of the Atomic Energy Industry,* August 1965, pp. 7–8.

There are a number of design problems which must be overcome before nuclear superheat can become practical. Some of these problems are (a) inadvertent flooding of superheat core steam passages causing significant reactivity changes, (b) the need to dry steam before it enters the superheat elements to prevent erosion and scaling, and (c) the need for improved performance and corrosion resistance of fuel cladding at high temperature.[45] Nevertheless, nuclear superheating is already included in at least five small prototype reactors,[46] and in the August 1965 Joint Committee on Atomic Energy Hearings three reactor manufacturers stated that they were actively engaged in developing superheat.

Table 5–11 shows the sensitivity of fuel cost to changes in thermal efficiency. It must be borne in mind that these results assume that no increase in enrichment (thus in consumption cost) is associated with increases in thermal efficiency; hence the results are somewhat academic. A change of 10 percent in thermal efficiency is associated with a change of 8.3 percent in fuel cost (when thermal efficiency varies from 31 to 39 percent). Or, in terms of thermal efficiency percentage points, a change of one percentage point causes a change of 2.5 percent in fuel cost.

Summary

In an attempt to summarize quickly these past two chapters, table 5–12 lists the elasticities of fuel cost with respect to each of the parameters discussed. A few words of caution are in order concerning the interpretation of the elasticities. The majority of the cost figures are based on engineering estimates. The purpose of the calculations is to give some quantitative description of the various factors influencing fuel cost. Although we feel that the estimates assumed are as valid as any that are available, they are nonetheless no more than estimates.

It is also important to guard against comparing the elasticities of the first five parameters with those of the last four. The last four parameters are not expressed in comparable units with the others (the first five parameters are cost while the last four are technical or percentages). It is meaningful, though, to observe that fuel cost is considerably more sensitive to the price of natural uranium and the cost of separative work than to the other *cost* components. And fabrication cost ranks next in importance: fuel cost is twice as sensitive to fabrication cost as to the plutonium credit or to reprocessing cost.

The high elasticities of thermal efficiency and exposure emphasize the

45. *Power*, March 1965, p. S–20.
46. *Electrical World*, 14 June 1965, p. 86.

Table 5-11. Sensitivity of fuel cost to variation in thermal efficiency (in mills per kilowatt-hour)

Thermal efficiency	Fuel cost	Enrichment (percentage U-235)	C	F	R	S	WC	P
.31	1.44 (100)	2.55	.85 (59)	.29 (20)	.19 (13)	.03 (2)	.26 (18)	.17 (−11)
.33	1.37 (100)	2.55	.80 (58)	.27 (20)	.18 (13)	.02 (2)	.24 (18)	.16 (−11)
.35	1.30 (100)	2.55	.75 (58)	.26 (20)	.18 (14)	.02 (2)	.23 (18)	.15 (−11)
.37	1.24 (100)	2.60	.71 (57)	.25 (20)	.18 (14)	.02 (2)	.22 (18)	.14 (−11)
.39	1.19 (100)	2.60	.68 (57)	.24 (20)	.17 (15)	.02 (2)	.21 (17)	.13 (−11)
.41	1.14 (100)	2.60	.64 (57)	.23 (20)	.17 (15)	.02 (2)	.20 (17)	.12 (−11)
.43	1.09 (100)	2.60	.61 (56)	.22 (20)	.17 (16)	.02 (2)	.19 (17)	.12 (−11)

Note: Percentages given in parentheses: C = consumption, F = fabrication, R = reprocessing, S = shipping, WC = working capital, P = plutonium credit.

Assumptions: Natural uranium, $6 per pound of U_3O_8; separative work cost, $30 per kilogram; plutonium credit, $7 per gram; shipping cost, $5 per kilogram; interest on working capital, 10 percent; plant factor, 80 percent. Fabrication and reprocessing cost assumed to vary with throughputs of those facilities: for example, with nuclear industry of 15,000 megawatts and fuel enriched to 2.656 percent, fabrication cost is $56.50 per kilogram and reprocessing is $38 per kilogram.

Table 5–12. Summary of elasticities of fuel cost with respect to parameters

Parameter	Parameter range From	To	Elasticity of fuel cost with respect to parameter	Source of cost data, table number
Cost of separative work	$24	$30	0.36	4–10
Natural uranium price	$ 6	$ 8	0.35	4–9
Fabrication cost[a]	80%	100%	0.22	5–2
Plutonium price	$ 7	$ 9	−0.11	5–8
Reprocessing cost[a]	80%	100%	0.09	5–4
Thermal efficiency	31%	39%	−0.83	5–11
Exposure	80%	100%	−0.85	5–9
Working capital interest rate	7%	10%	0.16	5–6
Capacity of nuclear industry	12,000MW	15,000MW	−0.15	5–5

[a]Fabrication and reprocessing costs are varied from 80 percent to 100 percent of cost functions specified in the reference tables.

Formula:
$$\text{Elasticity} = \frac{\dfrac{FC_2 - FC_1}{FC_2 + FC_1}}{\dfrac{P_2 - P_1}{P_2 + P_1}}$$

where
$$FC = \text{fuel cost}$$
$$P = \text{parameter value.}$$

large potential for cost reduction inherent in those technical factors. The cost of increasing either of the factors, however, must be less than the resulting saving. The working capital interest rate, though not negligible, is certainly not critical. The significant economies of scale in fabrication and reprocessing are highlighted by the nuclear capacity elasticity, a source of fuel cost reduction resulting only from the growth of the industry, assuming a constant technology.

Chapter 6. Uranium

Future uranium prices are important inputs for our benefit-cost model. Benefits are measured as the differences in energy costs of light water and advanced converter nuclear plants. Changes in uranium prices have different relative impacts on energy costs of these two types of plants. "A given increase in the cost of natural uranium increases the cost of energy from current types of light water reactors twice as much as it increases that of the advanced thermal reactors."[1] As calculated in chapter 4, a change of 10 percent in the price of natural uranium is associated with a change of 3.5 percent in the fuel cost of light water reactors, and consequently, about a change of 1.8 percent in advanced converter fuel cost.

Before proceeding with our analysis of uranium, we should mention briefly the other raw material which can serve as fuel in nuclear plants. Our representative advanced converter, the high-temperature, gas-cooled reactor, uses a thorium cycle. Thorium is the main fertile material in lieu of uranium-238. Therefore, the fission of uranium-235 produces uranium-233 as a "by-product" rather than plutonium. We shall assume that uranium-233 is burned in a subsequent fuel cycle, thereby reducing uranium makeup requirements. We shall therefore not examine thorium reserves but shall accept the AEC statement that "reasonably assured resources of thorium in the United States are more than ample to meet foreseeable requirements." Also, "total thorium requirements for nuclear use in the next 15 years probably will be measured only in hundreds of tons," whereas there are possibly some 500,000 tons of resources in the United States on the basis of up to $10 per pound of thoria ($ThO_2$).[2]

Description of the Uranium Industry

The supply side of the domestic uranium industry includes the mining of uranium ore and the milling operations necessary to separate uranium con-

1. U.S. Atomic Energy Commission, *Analysis of Advanced Converters and Self-Sustaining Breeders,* reprinted in *AEC Authorizing Legislation, Fiscal Year 1966, Part 3,* March 1965, p. 1762. Referred to hereafter as *Analysis of Advanced Converters.*
2. U.S. Atomic Energy Commission, *Annual Report to Congress of the Atomic Energy Commission for 1965,* January 1966, p. 72.

centrate. As of 1966 the demand side consists almost entirely of the AEC.[3] Although private power companies may buy uranium, it is doubtful if this right will be significantly exercised until 1969. The reason is that enriched, not natural, uranium is needed for most reactors in the United States. Enrichment facilities, as discussed in chapter 4, are controlled by the AEC, and the AEC will not enrich domestic, privately owned uranium until 1969.[4]

The AEC has been procuring uranium primarily for weapons. At the present time, the installed nuclear capacity in the United States is only 1,000 megawatts, compared to about 200,000 megawatts of conventional thermal capacity. The amount of uranium leased to civilian reactor operators is only 13 percent of annual AEC purchases.[5] The AEC procurement program for uranium will terminate in 1970. It was originally scheduled to terminate in 1966, but because it was believed that the effect on uranium suppliers would be harmful, a "stretchout" program was improvised. Some deliveries under existing contracts were shifted from 1962–1966 to 1966–1970. And of those deliveries shifted forward, an equal additional amount will be purchased at a lower price. The price will have an upper limit of about $6.75 per pound in that period compared to the $8.00 per pound price which was announced in 1956.[6]

Over the past several years the United States has been the largest producer of uranium in the free world. Production comes from more than twenty uranium mills, ranging in capacity from 300 tons to more than 3,000 tons of ore per day. The ore has consistently averaged around 0.25 percent U_3O_8, i.e., 5 pounds of U_3O_8 per ton of ore.

These mills are supplied by several hundred mines which also vary widely in size and cost of production.[7] Approximately 10 percent of the mines account for more than 80 percent of production, and 20 percent account for more than 90 percent.[8] The mines are about equally divided between open pit and deep underground operations.

3. As an exception, the *New York Times,* 27 March 1966, p. 1, reported three barter arrangements in which European utilities bought about 1,000 tons of domestic uranium at about $4 per pound. These utilities will exchange the natural uranium with the AEC for enriched uranium (and pay the AEC for enrichment costs). See also n. 4 below.

4. Some firms may not wait until 1969 to begin buying natural uranium if they anticipate a price rise. The *New York Times,* 7 April 1966, p. 1, states that Westinghouse and General Electric "are reported to be in the market for millions of pounds of uranium ore, looking forward to 1969." The *Wall Street Journal,* 1 August 1966, p. 9, reports that "at least six large orders from private concerns have been placed, most of them for delivery in 1968 and later."

5. The AEC *Annual Report for 1965,* p. 69, shows that purchases for 1965 were 13,140 tons of U_3O_8. A table in U.S. Atomic Energy Commission, *Estimated Growth of Civilian Nuclear Power,* Report TID-4500, March 1965, p. 16, indicates that about 1,750 tons of natural uranium were needed in 1965 to provide enriched uranium for United States civilian power.

6. AEC, *Annual Report for 1965,* pp. 69–70.

7. *Private Ownership of Special Nuclear Materials, 1964,* p. 160.

8. J. Hogerton, L. Geller, and A. Gerber, *The Outlook for Uranium: A Survey of the U.S. Uranium Market,* a report to the East Central Nuclear Group (New York: S. M. Stoller Associates, 1965), p. 7. Referred to hereafter as *Outlook for Uranium.*

The AEC stretchout program involves only ten uranium milling companies, but these companies own or control 80 percent of the AEC's 1965 estimate of low-cost uranium reserves.[9] Clearly, a number of mills must either phase out of business or merge with other firms. Four mills discontinued operations in 1965.[10]

Table 6–1 presents a crude estimate of the combined capacity utilization rate of uranium mills which will participate in the stretchout program, viz., 71 percent. The nominal capacity figures given are based upon a number of assumptions and are not accurate indicators of maximum production capability. One analysis has estimated that the utilization rate, based upon maximum capacity, will be 50–60 percent.[11] It is possible that some of the firms phasing out of business will be merged with firms listed in the table, further understating capacities. Consolidation would appear likely because of the large amount of capacity which is excluded from the stretchout program: 22,500 tons of ore per day was the total mill capacity in 1961 compared to 15,200 tons per day owned by the ten companies participating in the stretchout.

The cost of producing U_3O_8 varies considerably, depending upon the type of uranium deposit and the distance to the mill.[12] A breakdown of the cost for one particular uranium producer is instructive in illustrating the relative importance of various components. Table 6–2 is such a breakdown for an unidentified producer. Variable cost appears to be about $3.20 per pound, or slightly less than half total cost. This rate squares with the recent $4 per pound sales to European utilities, reportedly at incremental costs.

As is any extractive industry, uranium is an industry of increasing costs. That is, the less the output, the more it can be drawn from lower-cost nearby high-quality sources, while the greater the output, the more it must be drawn from high-cost distant low-quality sources.

The role of reserves is critical to an understanding of the economics of the industry. A minimum reserve requirement is necessary to meet the production schedule, and there is certainly an upper limit to reserves beyond which further exploration investment is not profitable. Another important characteristic of reserves is the random element in the relation between market price, exploratory effort, and increases in deposits. The analogy quoted below is a good description of the short history of the uranium industry.

9. Ibid., p. 10.
10. AEC, *Annual Report for 1965*, p. 71.
11. *Outlook for Uranium*, p. 10.
12. The *Wall Street Journal*, 1 August 1966, p. 9, states that "knowledgeable mining authorities estimate that a company must spend at least $1,200,000 on exploration and development before it will be able to begin producing uranium from a deposit 700 feet down, compared with $800,000 for a deposit 200 feet down."

Table 6–1. Uranium mills participating in 1966–1970 AEC stretchout procurement program

Company	Average tons U_3O_8 delivery per year[a]	Nominal capacity in tons U_3O_8 per year[b]	Average capacity factor-percentage[c]
Anaconda	745	2,250	33
Atlas	950	1,130	84
Federal-Radorock	362	375	97
Homestake-Sapin	1,080	1,700	120[d]
Kerr-McGee	1,520	2,480	61
Union Carbide (Wyo.)	200	375	53
Union Carbide (Colo.)	960	1,500	64
United Nuclear	955	—[d]	—[d]
Utah Construction	524	750	70
Vanadium	312	225	138
Western Nuclear	536	640	84
Total	8,144	11,425	71[e]

[a]U.S. Atomic Energy Commission, *Annual Report to Congress of the Atomic Energy Commission for 1965*, January 1966, p. 70, gives total deliveries for each company. Average per year was obtained by dividing by five years.

[b]Nominal capacities in tons of ore per day were obtained from J. Hogerton, L. Geller, and A. Gerber, *The Outlook for Uranium: A Survey of the U.S. Uranium Market*, a report for the East Central Nuclear Group (New York: S. M. Stroller Associates, 1965), p. 12, and AEC *Annual Report for 1961*, p. 177. Conversion into capacities expressed in tons of U_3O_8 per year was accomplished by assuming 300 operating days per year and 0.25 percent U_3O_8 in ore.

[c]Column 1 divided by column 2, multiplied by 100.

[d]United Nuclear's ores to be treated in Homestake-Sapin Mill.

[e]Column 1 total divided by column 2 total.

This randomness means that the industry's response to higher or lower price is inherently awkward and sticky. It operates like an automobile with a worn and rusted accelerator pedal. The driver may apply a modest additional pressure, with no result; additional pressure, still no more speed; only a little more pressure and the car shoots forward as though jet-propelled. The driver releases pressure, but the speed continues just as great; still less pressure, but the same speed; a little less, and suddenly he barely crawls.[13]

Two major elements determine the size of reserves needed. The first is the time period required to delineate and develop discovered deposits, install surface and underground mine plants, and bring the mines to production.

13. M. A. Adelman, *The Supply and Price of Natural Gas*, Supplement to the *Journal of Industrial Economics* (Oxford: Basil Blackwell, 1962), p. 22.

Table 6-2. Breakdown of costs for unidentified uranium producer (underground mining)

Item	Cost (dollars per pound U_3O_8) Range	Average
Land or royalty cost	$0.30–0.50	$0.40
Exploration cost	0.60–1.00	0.80
Development and mining cost	1.95–2.45	2.20
Milling cost	0.75–1.25	1.00
Administrative cost	0.10–0.30	0.20
Allowance for amortization	0.75–1.25	1.00
Gross return on capital		1.40
Total		$7.00

Note: Line items include taxes other than federal income taxes.
Source: Outlook for Uranium, p. 36.

The AEC estimates that an average time should be four to six years.[14] The second element determining the size of reserves is the estimated average time required for prospecting and exploration effort to find new deposits. Of course this is the element in which a random factor may play an important role, and indeed the average time for an individual prospector may be from a few months to never. But in considering the collective efforts of all prospectors in the industry, an average time is more meaningful.

The early experience of the industry indicates that the average time for discovery was very long, although certain factors may shorten the time. These factors include a better knowledge of uranium geology and exploration methods, and experienced men and organizations. As a best estimate, the AEC has predicted four to six years.[15] Thus, if we assume four to six years as the time to develop new deposits and bring them to production, and four to six years as the time necessary to discover new deposits and explore them, the adequate industry reserve at any given time should be eight to twelve times the production rate.[16]

The quality of reserves discovered is important. Even if huge reserves are found, the cost of extracting the U_3O_8 from the reserves may be high. The quality is crucial therefore insofar as the long-run supply of uranium is con-

14. Allan E. Jones, manager, Grand Junction Office, AEC, remarks to the Ninth Annual Minerals Symposium, Moab, Utah, May 1964, reprinted in *Private Ownership of Special Nuclear Materials, 1964,* p. 180.
15. Ibid., p. 181.
16. For a different estimate, see *Outlook for Uranium,* p. 18, in which a seven-year lead time is suggested.

100

cerned, and there is little evidence available on which decisions can be based.

Although the description of the industry so far has been limited to the United States, some remarks should be directed to the world industry. The 1964 Private Fuels Ownership Law has, in essence, excluded suppliers from outside the United States from competition for domestic markets until at least 1975. The law provides that the AEC will not toll-enrich foreign uranium if it is to be sold to domestic reactor operators.[17] Yet domestic suppliers may compete in the world market.

Canadian uranium production has ranked second to the United States in the free world. Canadian uranium is produced by a few large mining and milling operations. Compared to the American ore reserves, Canadian reserves are lower grade, but because of the economies of scale, Canadian unit costs are roughly comparable to United States costs.[18] Nearly all Canadian sales have been to the governments of the United States and the United Kingdom. But "production has been declining and will continue to do so from a rate of 7,587 tons of U_3O_8 in 1963 to a rate of approximately 1,200 tons per year starting in 1967 through 1971. Only one Canadian producer is expected to be in operation in 1970."[19]

South Africa is the third largest producer of uranium. As in Canada, almost all sales are made under long-term contracts to the United States and United Kingdom governments. Sales under these contracts are expected to decline from the 4,500 tons of U_3O_8 produced in 1963 to approximately 1,000 tons per year in the early seventies. South African uranium occurs in gold ores, which permits much of the uranium to be produced as a joint product. Only two or three mills will produce uranium under government contracts in the 1970–1973 period. It is generally believed that these mills can produce uranium at costs substantially less than that attained by the lowest-cost producers in the United States or Canada.[20]

Other free world countries with significant reserves are France, Australia, and Spain. French reserves should permit production at the current annual rate of 2,000 tons of U_3O_8 for many years. Some authorities consider it unlikely that French uranium will be a major factor in markets outside the

17. Specifically, the AEC is directed by the legislation not to offer toll-enrichment service on foreign material intended for use in domestic reactors "to the extent necessary to assure maintenance of a viable domestic uranium industry." The AEC had originally proposed that protection should extend to no later than 1 July 1975 (*Nucleonics*, 22 [September 1964]: 18).

18. Atomic Industrial Forum, *A Study of the Possible Effects of Private Ownership of Nuclear Fuels and Toll Enrichment on Uranium Markets*, April 1964, reprinted in *Private Ownership of Special Nuclear Materials, 1964*, p. 160.

19. Ibid.

20. Ibid., p. 161.

Table 6–3. Estimated Reserves of U_3O_8 in 1971

Country	Tons U_3O_8	Price per pound
United States	95,600	$8 or less
Canada	190,000	$10 or less
South Africa	137,000	$8 or less
Others	56,000	$10 or less

Sources: Atomic Industrial Forum, *A Study of the Possible Effects of Private Ownership of Nuclear Fuels and Toll Enrichment on Uranium Markets,* April 1964, reprinted in *Private Ownership of Special Nuclear Materials,* 1964, p. 159. Also, *Outlook for Uranium,* p. 17.

Common Market for the near term.[21] Australian production is also likely to offer only minor competition in the early seventies. Spanish reserves have recently been estimated at 10,000 tons of U_3O_8, but unless reserves are increased substantially, Spanish production will be small.[22]

As a rough comparison of the major uranium countries, the estimated reserves of U_3O_8 are listed in table 6–3, assuming no further additions to reserves and that known procurement contracts are carried out.

Historical Development

The United States government established its first uranium purchase program in 1948. An assessment was made of all known sources in the free world. Known major sources were the Eldorado Mine at Great Bear in Canada, the Shinkolobwe Mine in the Congo, the gold deposits of South Africa, and the vanadium deposits of the Colorado Plateau.[23] All of these, except the South African deposits, had produced uranium for the Manhattan Project.

Production prior to 1948 amounted to 10,156 tons of U_3O_8 from foreign sources and 1,435 tons from domestic sources.[24] The production capability of the then known sources was only a small proportion of needs. Therefore, contracts for production from the known sources were made. The degree of dependence on foreign sources is illustrated by the fact that from 1948 through 1956 domestic deliveries were 10,797 tons of U_3O_8, or only 28 percent of total deliveries.[25]

An interesting way to examine the development of the uranium industry

21. Ibid.
22. Ibid.
23. Allan E. Jones, manager, Grand Junction Office, AEC, remarks to the Ninth Annual Minerals Symposium, Moab, Utah, May 1964, reprinted in *Private Ownership of Special Nuclear Materials, 1964,* p. 178.
24. Ibid.
25. Ibid.

Table 6–4. Deliveries of U_3O_8 to AEC and domestic reserves (in tons of U_3O_8)

Fiscal year	Domestic deliveries actual and scheduled	Total deliveries actual and scheduled	Domestic reserves[a]
1948	116	2,011	2,500
1949	115	2,241	2,500
1950	323	3,063	5,000
1951	639	3,686	5,000
1952	824	3,657	5,000
1953	982	2,887	10,000
1954	1,455	4,693	17,500
1955	2,141	5,940	22,000
1956	4,202	10,434	68,000
1957	7,582	16,156	105,000
1958	10,243	26,375	205,000
1959	15,162	33,327	222,000
1960	16,566	34,581	240,000
1961	17,758	32,260	230,000
1962	17,255	29,362	171,000[b]
1963	15,760	26,982	165,000
1964	12,200	18,250	159,000
1965	11,600	15,650	—
1966	10,500	12,800	—
1967	8,900	9,850	—
1968	7,800	7,800	—
1969	7,800	7,800	—
1970	7,800	7,800	—
1971	3,900	3,900	—

[a]Domestic reserves are estimated at $8 per pound of U_3O_8.

[b]The large decrease from 1961 to 1962 is superficial. A reevaluation of the original 1962 estimate of 210,000 tons resulted in a revised estimate of 171,000 tons, and a "paper loss" of 39,000 tons.

Source: Allan E. Jones, manager, Grand Junction Office, AEC, remarks to the Ninth Annual Minerals Symposium Uranium Section, Moab, Utah, May 1964, reprinted in *Private Ownership of Special Nuclear Materials, 1964,* p. 183.

is by noting AEC comments on criticisms of their past procurement practices, criticisms such as the following:

Two past mistakes of the AEC have added to the difficulty of the transition. The first occurred in the late forties and early fifties when the AEC, under-estimating the amount of domestic uranium available and impelled by the urgency of its need, entered into long-term contracts that from 1957 to 1963 required it to buy more than 50% of its ore from

103

foreign sources at prices higher than those paid for domestic ore. By 1966 these contracts will have brought 141,000 tons of U_3O_8 to the United States and sent $2.9 billion to foreign producers.

The second mistake was the AEC's reluctance to cut back its domestic buying program soon enough. As early as 1956 it was becoming evident that the uranium boom had gotten out of hand and the Government was going to be swamped with ore. It was not until 1958, however, that the AEC took definite steps to discourage exploration for new deposits of uranium.[26]

In order for us to appreciate the arguments better, table 6-4 provides information on actual and scheduled U_3O_8 deliveries to the AEC from 1947 to 1971, as well as estimated United States reserves.

To the first criticism, the AEC stated that it had carefully considered all available information in 1947, and only 2,500 tons of economic reserves were known of at that time in the United States. Nevertheless, the AEC believed that greater optimism for the potential of the United States was justified, and it established a program to stimulate prospecting.[27]

In answer to the second criticism, the AEC has given the following explanation:

In May 1956 the AEC issued the announcement of its program from 1962 through 1966 as a stimulus for continued exploration to develop adequate reserves for defense needs. Known reserves at that time were only about 70,000 tons of U_3O_8 and exploration had already shown signs of stopping in the absence of an assured market beyond March 31, 1962, the termination date of the original ore buying program. Known domestic reserves at the beginning of 1956, taken in conjunction with projected production from foreign sources, were insufficient to meet established procurement objectives. In these circumstances AEC could have been justly criticized had it not taken steps to provide for continued exploration and development.

This announcement in May 1956 stimulated a new wave of prospecting and exploration with results which, for the first time, indicated that the United States might become independent of foreign supplies of this strategic commodity. However, the extent to which reserves would be increased by this activity could not be determined for some time.

On November 24, 1958, the AEC removed the open-end feature of the May 1956 announcement to guard against serious overproduction should additional very large uranium discoveries be made. As of that time, however, the quantity of uranium which the AEC expected to receive through 1966 did not exceed projected requirements. As late as November 1962 it appeared that the program commitments, including

26. Harold B. Meyers, "The Great Uranium Glut," *Fortune*, February 1964, p. 108.
27. U.S. Congress, Joint Committee on Atomic Energy, *AEC Authorizing Legislation, Fiscal Year 1965, Part 1*, 88th Congress, 2nd Session, March 1964, p. 218.

stretchout arrangements, would result in reasonable balance of supply with requirements through 1970. The recent decision to reduce production of fissionable materials, however, will result in an interim imbalance in uranium supply versus demand.[28]

Without attempting to make a judgment on whether the AEC was justified in its actions, it is instructive to observe the behavior of reserves. Although exploration activities were well underway by 1950, it was not until the mid-fifties that additions to reserves became large. And in the two-year period 1956–1957, reserves increased explosively by about 130,000 tons. The main factor was the delineation of deposits in the Ambrosia Lake area of New Mexico and the Gas Hills area of Wyoming.[29] After the 1958 announcement by the AEC that purchase commitments would be limited to ore bodies already developed, additions to reserves almost ceased, and "since 1959, exploration and development activity has been largely dormant."[30] We should point out, however, that there are indications in 1966 that this activity is rapidly reviving.[31]

In the next section, we shall make projections of the demand for uranium under various assumptions about the growth of nuclear power capacity. These projections will be compared with uranium reserves in an effort to make some judgments as to the probable trend of uranium prices.

Future Demand for Uranium

Since the AEC procurement program ends in 1970, the major demand for uranium after that date should be by nuclear power plant operators. Domestic producers are protected from foreign competition for domestic requirements and may be able to capture some fraction of foreign requirements, but the amount of foreign demand they may capture is quite uncertain and will depend upon political factors in addition to comparative costs. For this analysis, therefore, we shall concentrate on estimating domestic requirements.

Two basic elements must be considered in our demand projection: (a) the time path of installed nuclear capacity and (b) the uranium consumption characteristics of the types of plants installed. We shall discuss the capacity projection in some detail, since it is important not only for projecting uranium requirements but also for calculating advanced converter benefits. A computer program has been written which enables us to project uranium requirements for a number of different assumptions. After making those projections,

28. Ibid., p. 219.
29. *Outlook for Uranium*, p. 18.
30. Ibid.
31. The *Wall Street Journal*, 1 August 1966, p. 9, states that "producers are scouring the U.S. West—and parts of other countries, too—in a feverish search for ore. . . . Western Nuclear has quadrupled its holdings in the past six months leasing or claiming 50,000 acres in Wyoming and Colorado."

we shall compare them with known reserves and make a judgment about future uranium prices.

Growth of nuclear capacity. Predictions of the growth of nuclear capacity are numerous and vary considerably. Table 6–5 lists some of these predictions. We shall use the AEC estimate (approximated by an equation) as a reference for our analysis and vary the rate of growth implied by that estimate. The two main reasons for this selection are (*a*) that the AEC 1980 estimate is roughly at the mid-point of the other estimates, being neither overly optimistic nor overly pessimistic, and (*b*) that we do not have the resources to make an independent estimate.

We should emphasize that the following discussion on growth projection is basically to point out the difficulties of such projection and the vast margin for error. A striking illustration of the uncertainty involved in growth projections is provided by an estimate of nuclear capacity made by two AEC officials in 1957. Their estimate for 1980 nuclear capacity was 227,200 megawatts, or about three times the 1980 capacity estimate we shall use in this analysis.[32]

Generally, predictions are first made of the total energy consumption expected in the future, followed by estimates of the share of energy supply captured by producers of electricity. Finally, predictions of the growth of nuclear capacity are based upon estimates of the share of the market nuclear plants will capture. We shall not discuss the methods of projection used to estimate the total energy and total electricity time paths, since a paper given in 1964 at the Third International Conference on the Peaceful Uses of Atomic Energy provides a summary of projections by various groups and contains a good bibliography of the relevant literature.[33]

If we take a certain growth of total electric power capacity as given, the share of that growth captured by nuclear capacity is dependent upon the investment decisions of power producers. Clearly, the only "correct" way to estimate the nuclear share is through a detailed region-by-region examination of the comparative costs of nuclear, conventional thermal, and hydro power. This approach has been followed by a number of groups listed in table 6–5.[34]

32. Kenneth Davis and Louis H. Roddis, Jr., "A Projection of Nuclear Power Costs," in National Industrial Conference Board report, *Fifth Annual Conference: Atomic Energy in Industry,* 1957, p. 25. It is interesting that in 1969 the AEC estimate of 1980 capacity had risen to 150,000 megawatts!

33. James Tape, F. Pittman, and M. Searl, "Future Energy Needs and the Role of Nuclear Power," paper given at the Third United Nations International Conference on the Peaceful Uses of Atomic Energy, Geneva, August 1964.

34. See the Arthur D. Little report, *Outlook for Central-Station Nuclear Power in the United States,* and the AEC report, *Estimated Growth of Civilian Nuclear Power,* March 1965.

Table 6–5. Nuclear capacity projections by various groups

Group	Nuclear capacity in 1980, thousands of megawatts			Nuclear share of total power capacity in 1980			Nuclear capacity in 2000, thousands of megawatts			Nuclear share of total power capacity in 2000		
	Low	Med	High	Low	Med	High	Low	Med	High	Low	Med	High
This analysis[a]	65.3	74.0	83.9	.13	.14	.16	513.8	732.9	1045.2	.31	.44	.63
AEC[b]	61.0	75.0	92.0	–	–	–	–	730.0	–	–	.44	–
Stoller Associates[c]	–	73.0	–	–	.14	–	500.0	600.0	700.0	–	.45	–
Westinghouse[d]	43.0	63.5	84.0	–	–	–	–	–	–	–	–	–
General Electric[d]	–	87.3	–	–	–	–	–	–	–	–	–	–
Federal Power Commission[e]	–	70.0	–	–	–	–	–	–	–	–	–	–
Philip Sporn[e]	–	45.0	–	–	–	–	–	–	–	–	–	–
A. D. Little, Inc.[f]	–	64.0	–	–	–	–	–	–	–	–	–	–

[a]Table 6–7 gives basis for projection. Total power capacity in 1980 taken as 523.0 gigawatts (Federal Power Commission, *National Power Survey, 1964, Part I*, p. 215); in 2000, taken as 1,651.8 gigawatts (*AEC Appendices to a Report to the President, 1962*, p. 66).
[b]Mean capacities for 1980 and 2000 taken from AEC report given as Appendix 5 to *AEC Authorizing Legislation, Fiscal Year 1966, Part 3*.
[c]*Outlook for Uranium*, p. 24.
[d]Joint Committee on Atomic Energy, *Development, Growth, and State of the Atomic Energy Industry*, August 1965, pp. 11, 38.
[e]Cited in *Outlook for Uranium*, pp. 24–25.
[f]Arthur D. Little, Inc., *The Outlook for Central-Station Nuclear Power in the United States*, September 1964, p. 17.

107

The investment decision of a power producer as to the choice of a nuclear or nonnuclear plant must be at the heart of any projection. Each producer has a different set of circumstances: capacity increment required; power system characteristics; availability of low-cost coal, oil, gas or hydro sites; nuclear safety considerations depending upon population density; air pollution concern (public pressure may soon make this property a significant nuclear cost advantage); and even geological considerations (a proposed nuclear plant in California was canceled in 1964 because of its proximity to the San Andreas fault). In addition, there are other less easily identifiable reasons for selecting a nuclear plant: prestige, training of personnel, and a bargaining weapon in dealing with fossil fuel suppliers.

A power producer must evaluate and compare the present value of the lifetime increment to total system cost for each alternative type of capacity addition. This prescription is more difficult to apply than it may appear, for the uncertainty surrounding nuclear cost estimates is much greater than for conventional plants, and some method of allowing for this must be employed to obtain comparable costs (e.g., discounting for uncertainty). Also, a kilowatt of nuclear capacity is not equivalent to a kilowatt of conventional capacity. The availabilities may differ. Nuclear capacity is generally superior to conventional capacity in its ability to respond to system load fluctuations more rapidly. The ultimate nuclear "stretch" capacity, discussed in chapter 3, is an unknown though highly important phenomenon. Stretch is smaller and more predictable in conventional thermal plants.

One approach to this decision is by computer simulation of the power system, in which a computer is used to simulate the expansion of the system, employing alternative patterns of capacity additions. An advantage of this method over the usual partial analysis is that it attempts to account for the effect of each alternative upon system dispatch, reserve requirements, and timing of future capacity additions; hence, the effect upon system cost over time.

> Frequently nuclear-plant economic evaluations are made simply by comparing total energy cost with that of the best conventional steam units available. In this type of computation, full-load costs are assumed, some plant capacity factor, . . . and the mills/kwhr. of the two alternative units are computed very simply. Such a comparison is far from complete, for it neglects many systems considerations, the effects on other units, the dynamic situation in time as costs change and other units are installed. . . .[35]

35. C. J. Baldwin et al., "Economic Aspects of System Expansion with Nuclear Units," *Power Apparatus and Systems*, February 1963, p. 2.

Another technique for power systems analysis is mathematical programming. While simulation permits the planner to try many alternative patterns, it is unlikely that the planner will evaluate every possible pattern. Mathematical programming is superior in this respect. A linear programming model can be formulated in which a systematic search is made over all alternatives to determine the joint investment and operating optimum. The unknowns are the capacities and operating levels of each type of plant (conventional, nuclear, hydro, etc.). The objective is to find those values of the unknowns which minimize total system cost subject to a number of constraints, e.g., peak demand and annual power demand.[36]

Obviously, it would be impossible for anyone concerned with predicting the growth of nuclear capacity in the United States to construct simulation models or mathematical programming models of each power system. Although such a procedure is advisable for the individual power producer, it is only practical to employ the less sophisticated single-unit comparisons in projecting total capacity growth.

Table 6–6 lists average fossil fuel costs and installed steam generating capacity by regions of the United States. In order to compare nuclear costs with these figures, we must calculate the fossil fuel cost at which a given nuclear energy cost is equivalent. The basic condition is to equate the total cost of energy produced in both types of plants:

$$C_n + c_n + OM_n = C_f + c_f + OM_f, \tag{6–1}$$

or

$$c_f = C_n + c_n + OM_n - C_f - OM_f. \tag{6–2}$$

And to convert c_f from mills per kilowatt-hour to cents per million Btu's,

$$c'_f = (c_f)(TE)/.03412 \tag{6–3}$$

where c'_f = fossil fuel cost equivalent to nuclear cost in cents per million Btu's

C = capital cost in mills per kilowatt-hour

c = fuel cost in mills per kilowatt-hour

OM = operation and maintenance cost in mills per kilowatt-hour

TE = thermal efficiency.

(The subscripts n and f represent nuclear and fossil fuel respectively.)

36. For an exposition of linear programming applied to power system planning, see Pierre Massé, *Optimal Investment Decisions: Rules for Action and Criteria for Choice* (Englewood Cliffs, N.J.: Prentice-Hall, 1962), pp. 160–197, 373–392. And, for an exposition of both computer simulation techniques and mathematical programming, see Thomas H. Naylor and John M. Vernon, *Microeconomics and Decision Models of the Firm* (New York: Harcourt, Brace and World, 1969).

109

As an illustration, consider the capital and operation and maintenance costs of a modern 800-megawatt coal plant estimated by Philip Sporn as of January 1966:[37]

$$C_f = 2.00 \text{ mills per kilowatt-hour}$$
$$OM_f = 0.30 \text{ mills per kilowatt-hour.}$$

(An 80 percent plant factor, 12.5 percent fixed charges, and 38.8 percent thermal efficiency are assumed.)

Sporn's nuclear cost estimates, also based upon an 800-megawatt unit, are:

$$C_n = 2.20 \text{ mills per kilowatt-hour}$$
$$c_n = 1.82 \text{ mills per kilowatt-hour}$$
$$OM_n = 0.40 \text{ mills per kilowatt-hour.}$$

(Nuclear liability insurance of 0.10 mills per kilowatt-hour is included in OM_n.)

Inserting these values into equations 6–2 and 6–3 gives:

$$c'_f = 24 \text{ cents per million Btu's.}$$

Referring to table 6–6, the January 1966 Sporn estimate of 24 cents would indicate that nuclear power could offer an economic alternative to

Table 6–6. 1964 fossil fuel costs and installed steam power capacity in the United States

Region	Average cost, cents per million Btu's	Steam power capacity, thousands of megawatts
New England	33.9	6.8
Middle Atlantic	27.5	28.0
East North Central	24.5	42.5
West North Central	25.2	11.9
South Atlantic	27.0	26.7
East South Central	19.7	17.5
West South Central	19.4	21.2
Mountain	22.7	6.5
Pacific	32.0	14.5
United States	25.3	176.3

Source: Edison Electric Institute, *Statistical Yearbook of the Electric Utility Industry for 1964,* New York, September 1965, pp. 7, 47.

power producers in all but three regions. If 24 cents were selected as the best current estimate of nuclear cost, the next step in predicting nuclear capacity growth would be to make some estimate of the nuclear fraction of

37. Sporn, 1966, p. 24.

capacity additions in those competitive areas. The figure of 24 cents is valid only for large plants; for smaller capacity additions nuclear plants are considerably less attractive.

Calculating the fossil fuel cost equivalents of the reference light water nuclear costs to be used in our benefit-cost analysis will also be instructive. Equations 6-2 and 6-3 require that we know capital and operation and maintenance costs, and thermal efficiency, for comparable conventional plants. Unfortunately, estimates of such information for conventional plants in 1975 and 1985 (dates for which we have estimated nuclear costs — see chapter 7) are not available. Consequently, we shall use Sporn's figures for the 800-megawatt coal plant. To make some adjustment for the differences in time and capacity (our nuclear estimates are for 1,000-megawatt plants), we shall arbitrarily reduce Sporn's figures by 5 percent.[38] Hence, the total energy cost of a 1,000-megawatt light water nuclear plant would be 3.79 mills per kilowatt-hour in 1975 and 3.32 mills per kilowatt-hour in 1985. The equivalent fossil fuel cost would be 19 cents per million Btu's in 1975 and 14 cents per million Btu's in 1985.

Obviously, one cannot compare the 1975 and 1985 nuclear costs with current fossil fuel costs, but the low level of our nuclear estimates does give a rough indication of the target fossil fuel suppliers will have to work toward to remain competitive. Cost reducing innovations in fossil fuels have been significant recently; the coal industry has increased the tonnage output per man by more than 50 percent in the past seven years.[39]

The introduction of the integral and unit train and other improvements in transporting coal by rail "have made possible savings of 30–50 percent in the price of transporting coal."[40] Another recent innovation which has reduced fossil fuel costs is the EHV (extra-high-voltage) transmission line.

38. Federal Power Commission, *National Power Survey, 1964, Part II*, p. 53, states that for conventional plants "it would appear that a reduction in cost per kilowatt will be increasingly difficult to achieve as size increases beyond the 500- to 750- megawatt range," although it also states that "some groups believe that decreasing costs, perhaps as much as $8 to $10 per kilowatt, may be achieved in going from 500- to 1000-megawatt units." A discussion of the assumptions underlying our nuclear cost estimates is given in chapter 7. Operation and maintenance and nuclear insurance costs for 1975 and 1985 were assumed to be .30 and .25 mills, respectively.

39. Louis H. Roddis, Jr., "The Atom: Catalyst for a 4-mill Kilowatt-hour," *Proceedings of the Atomic Industrial Forum, 1964*, 2 (December 1964): 79. Also, coal, which presently accounts for about 65 percent of the energy for thermal plants, is not in any sense about to be depleted. Coal reserves of the United States, as of 1960, on the basis of only 50 percent recovery, were 830 billion tons. The Federal Power Commission estimates that the total energy requirement of electric utilities in terms of coal equivalent will be approximately 900 million tons per year in 1980 (*National Power Survey, 1964, Part II*, p. 319).

40. Isabel H. Benham, "Can the Railroad and the Coal Industry Meet the Challenge of Lower Atomic Power Costs?", address before Cleveland Society of Security Analysts, 7 October 1964, p. 6.

Large power plants can be located at the coal mine, where transportation costs are nil. In effect, energy is transported in the form of electricity to distant consumption centers rather than in the form of coal. In one case, the costs of a 250-mile, 500-kilovolt EHV transmission line equated to 7–8 cents per million Btu's compared with the rates of 11–12 cents.[41]

During 1965, though, there have been some indications that the coal industry is abandoning its downward pressure on price.

> The pronouncements of many leaders of the coal industry in recent months have indicated that in their view the market for coal for electric generation has improved to the point where they can begin to consider significant increases in coal prices. How one can reconcile this view with a loss to the nuclear competitor of a market for the equivalent of 13,000,000 tons of coal per year *in one year* is rather difficult to understand — except on the generous assumption of an evaluation made in hope rather than fact.[42]

Clearly, any nuclear capacity projection must be highly uncertain. Uncertainty can be treated to some degree by varying the projection over a wide range, but even a "reasonably" wide range today may be insufficient because of unforeseen developments of tomorrow. Nevertheless, for any quantitative, and thus meaningful, analysis some growth projection must be assumed.

In order to employ the AEC projection efficiently in the computer program, a mathematical function was fitted to the yearly estimates. The resulting equation, which has a coefficient of determination of 0.999, is:

$$\text{cumulative capacity} = 21.05\ e^{\frac{1}{(4.0032\ +\ 0.1277t)}\,t} \qquad (6\text{--}4)$$

where $t = $ year number (1975 = 1, 1976 = 2, . . .).

One advantage of the equation is that it enables us to calculate the instantaneous rates of growth implied by the AEC projection. Table 6–7 lists for selected years the cumulative nuclear capacity and the implied nuclear capacity rate of growth. The explanation for the high rates in early years is that nuclear power will penetrate fossil fuel areas where the cost differential is large quite rapidly when the base nuclear capacity is small. After capturing these areas, the rate of nuclear capacity additions will slow down, approaching the rate of growth of total electrical capacity (the total use of electricity has increased at a remarkably steady rate over the last eighty years, with usage doubling approximately every ten years, or about 7 percent per year).[43]

41. Roddis, p. 79.
42. Sporn, 1966, p. 17.
43. Federal Power Commission, *National Power Survey, 1964, Part I*, p. 36.

Table 6–7. Nuclear capacity projections and rates of growth

(1) Year	(2) Instantaneous rate of growth of column 3	(3) Reference nuclear capacity, thousands of megawatts[a]	(4) Instantaneous rate of growth of column 5	(5) Nuclear capacity at 10 percent lower rate of growth, thousands of megawatts	(6) Instantaneous rate of growth of column 7	(7) Nuclear capacity at 10 percent higher rate of growth, thousands of megawatts
1975	0.24	26.8	0.22	26.1	0.27	27.4
1980	0.21	74.0	0.19	65.3	0.23	83.9
1985	0.18	160.9	0.17	131.3	0.20	197.2
1990	0.17	296.7	0.15	227.7	0.18	386.6
1995	0.15	486.9	0.13	355.6	0.16	666.6
2000	0.14	732.9	0.12	513.8	0.15	1045.2
2005	0.13	1033.0	0.11	699.9	0.14	1524.7

[a]The reference nuclear capacity, column 3, is computed by the equation:

$$\text{nuclear capacity} = 21.05\, e^{\frac{1}{4.0032 + 0.1277t}}$$
(thousands of megawatts)

where t = year number (1975 = 1, 1976 = 2, . . .).

Uranium requirements. The nuclear capacity projections discussed in the last section will now be combined with the uranium consumption characteristics of the reactors to calculate uranium requirements. Before proceeding, we should make our assumptions explicit. The uranium requirements which we calculate will be considered identical with the demand for uranium.[44] Since it is a rather unusual demand function which is not a function of its own price, an explanation is in order.

Uranium is demanded by nuclear plant operators who supply electricity. Doubling the uranium price should increase the cost of electricity by only about 12 percent. Because uranium is a necessary input and its cost is small relative to total power cost, an existing nuclear plant operator is likely to have a zero elasticity of demand for uranium. Also, as installed nuclear capacity grows, existing plant operators should increasingly dominate the demand for uranium relative to potential nuclear plant operators (who tend to contribute to a greater demand elasticity). However, current installed nuclear capacity is not large compared to potential capacity additions, and with nuclear and nonnuclear plants presently being close substitutes, the expected price of uranium can be critical to a decision to install a nuclear plant.

The mutual dependence of uranium price and nuclear capacity growth is impossible to ignore. It is clearly illogical to (*a*) assume a uranium price, (*b*) project nuclear capacity, (*c*) calculate uranium demand from projected capacity, and (*d*) determine uranium price by comparing demand with supply. The determined uranium price would only by chance be identical with the initially assumed price. The diagram below simplifies the issue. The arrows indicate the direction of influence, and the feedback from the price to nuclear capacity is represented by the dotted line.

$$\rightarrow \quad N \quad \rightarrow \quad D_u \quad \rightarrow \quad P_u \text{- - -}$$

where
N = nuclear capacity
D_u = demand for uranium
P_u = uranium price.

There are two possible escapes from the dilemma. First, we could assume that the price elasticity of demand for uranium is zero (in effect, breaking

44. Plutonium is expected to become a suitable fuel in light water reactors in the mid-seventies and in breeders in the mid-eighties. As discussed in chapter 5, plutonium supply can be either added to uranium supply or subtracted from uranium demand to study the nuclear fuels market. We have chosen the latter method; hence, our uranium requirements are net nuclear fuel requirements.

the dotted line), but as we have discussed previously, this is not reasonable. The second possible escape is simply to vary N over a reasonable range and study the effect on uranium price. This second alternative will, by necessity, be our choice.

Table 6–8 presents the major assumptions of the computer program used to calculate uranium requirements. Some of the estimates of inventory and makeup requirements are highly uncertain at this date, but unfortunately the scope of this analysis prevents us from making a sensitivity analysis of uranium requirements to changes in certain of the figures.[45]

Tables 6–9, 6–10, and 6–11 summarize the results of the analysis. Essentially, table 6–9 gives the result of the "standard" case and compares uranium requirements with reserves. The standard case assumes that nuclear capacity grows at the reference growth rate (see table 6–7) and that breeders are introduced in 1985. Uranium requirements are calculated both with and without advanced converters in the growth pattern (requirements with advanced converters in the pattern are shown in parentheses). Tables 6–10 and 6–11 give requirements for variations in the two major parameters: the nuclear capacity growth rate and the date of breeder introduction.

Although most of the assumptions made in calculating requirements are given in the tables, some further discussion is needed. One particularly important assumption relates to how the transition takes place from light water to advanced converter to uranium-235 fast breeder to plutonium fast breeder reactors. Clearly, each transition is similar to the transition from conventional to total nuclear, discussed earlier. The investment decision of the power producer lies at the heart of each. Since some assumption of the rate of each transition was necessary, we decided to make relatively simple ones (following the AEC in the *Analysis of Advanced Converters*). These assumptions were: (*a*) advanced converters would capture 10 percent of the total nuclear capacity addition in the first year, 20 percent in the second, etc.; (*b*) breeders would be introduced similarly, 10 percent of capacity addition in the first year, etc.; (*c*) of the total breeder capacity added, plutonium fast breeders would occupy that proportion permitted by available plutonium (produced in light water reactors initially, and later by breeders also); (*d*) any gap between total breeder capacity as defined by the transition rule and

---

45. *Outlook for Uranium* used figures which were generally somewhat lower than the AEC ones used in this analysis. The inventory requirement for plutonium breeders was especially lower: 3.0 kilograms per megawatt compared to AEC's 4.2 kilograms per megawatt. Using the lower figures for plutonium breeders, we calculated annual uranium requirements. A comparison with the annual requirements calculated in table 6–9 is as follows (requirements, in thousands of tons, using *Outlook for Uranium* assumptions given first): 1980, 15–15; 1990, 50–55; 1995, 63–78; 2000, 35–73; and 2005, 8–57. The lower plutonium requirements for breeders that *Outlook for Uranium* assumes permits a more rapid growth of plutonium breeders, which, in turn, reduces uranium requirements markedly.

Table 6-8. Assumptions of uranium consumption characteristics of different reactor types

Reactor	Inventory, short tons U_3O_8 Megawatt	Makeup, short tons U_3O_8 per megawatt-year	Plutonium production, kilograms megawatt-year
Light water	1.0[a] 0.7[b]	0.16[a] 0.13[c] 0.25[d]	0.32
Advanced converter (high-temperature, gas-cooled)	0.6	0.025	—[e]
Fast U-235 breeder	1.44	0.23	0.83
Fast plutonium breeder	4.2[f]	−0.43[g]	0.43[g]

[a] Applicable through 1976.
[b] Applicable after 1976.
[c] Applicable from 1977 until four years before breeder introduction.
[d] Applicable after four years before breeder introduction.
[e] Thorium is fertile material; hence, U-233 is produced rather than plutonium, and is assumed to be recycled.
[f] Kilograms of plutonium.
[g] Excess kilograms of plutonium after allowance for annual makeup.

Lead time assumptions: Uranium inventory and/or makeup in year t is a requirement in year t-1 (for mining, conversion, and fabrication). Four-year lead time from production of plutonium in converters until availability to breeders. Three-year lead time from production of plutonium in breeders until availability to breeders.

Source: U.S. Atomic Energy Commission, *Analysis of Advanced Converters and Self-Sustaining Breeders,* reprinted in *AEC Authorizing Legislation, Fiscal Year 1966, Part 3,* March 1965, p. 1751, and private communication from George Y. Jordy, coauthor of this AEC report.

plutonium breeder capacity would be filled with uranium-235 breeders; and (*e*) as plutonium availability permitted, plutonium breeders would displace uranium-235 breeders.

These assumptions are arbitrary and should be recognized as such. Many other transition rules could have been followed. For example, some view the fast uranium-235 breeder with much skepticism, and consequently a breeder transition completely determined by plutonium availability is more reasonable to them.

Two other assumptions should be mentioned. The fast plutonium breeders are assumed to use depleted uranium as the fertile material. Depleted uranium is the "by-product" of the AEC enrichment operation. As discussed

Table 6–9. Uranium requirements for power and reserves for reference nuclear capacity projections (in thousands of U_3O_8 short tons)

Requirements		
Year	Annual requirements[a]	Cumulative requirements from 1 January 1966[a]
1975	11 (10)	40 (39)
1980	18 (15)	103 (96)
1985	43 (25)	264 (201)
1990	72 (54)	524 (377)
1995	89 (78)	932 (711)
2000	82 (73)	1,365 (1,096)
2005	65 (57)	1,746 (1,432)

	Reserves	
Price range per pound U_3O_8	Reserves by category as of 1 January 1966[b]	Cumulative reserves over categories
$ 8 and under (reasonably assured)	133	133
$10 and under (estimated additional)	368	501
$10 to $15 (reasonably assured)	150	651
$10 to $15 (possible additional)	200	851
$15 to $30 (reasonably assured)	170	1,021
$15 to $30 (possible additional)	440	1,461

[a] Requirements with advanced converters in growth pattern are given in parentheses.

[b] Reserves are given in AEC *Annual Report for 1965*, p. 71. Reserves in $8 price range are given as 145,000 tons; we assumed AEC will stockpile 30,000 tons of procurement in U_3O_8 form (following *Outlook for Uranium*, p. 14) and thus added this amount to get 175,000 tons. AEC procurement over the period, 42,000 tons, was then subtracted to get 133,000 tons.

Assumptions: Breeder reactors introduced in 1985: 10 percent of capacity addition in 1985 is breeder, 20 percent in 1986, etc. (following AEC in *Analysis of Advanced Converters*); a total plant factor of .8 is applied through 1980, declining linearly to .7 in 1990, and .7 thereafter; plutonium is recycled in light water reactors through 1981, then no more; advanced converter transition follows same pattern as breeder transition, i.e., 10 percent in 1975, 20 percent in 1976, etc.; additional assumption given in table 6–8.

Table 6–10. Uranium requirements for power for two variations of reference nuclear capacity projection (in thousands of U_3O_8 short tons)

Year	Nuclear growth rate 10 percent lower than reference rate		Nuclear growth rate 10 percent greater than reference rate	
	Annual requirements	Cumulative requirements from 1 January 1966	Annual requirements	Cumulative requirements from 1 January 1966
1975	10 (9)	39 (34)	12 (11)	40 (40)
1980	15 (12)	94 (88)	22 (18)	113 (105)
1985	34 (19)	224 (174)	55 (33)	313 (234)
1990	51 (39)	415 (302)	100 (77)	665 (474)
1995	60 (52)	697 (531)	131 (117)	1,250 (959)
2000	52 (45)	983 (781)	128 (116)	1,905 (1,549)
2005	39 (32)	1,220 (985)	110 (98)	2,517 (2,100)

Note: Requirements with advanced converters in growth pattern are given in parentheses.

Assumptions: Breeder reactors introduced in 1985: 10 percent of capacity addition in 1985 is breeder, 20 percent in 1986, etc. (following AEC in *Analysis of Advanced Converters*); a total plant factor of .8 is applied through 1980, declining linearly to .7 in 1990, and .7 thereafter; plutonium is recycled in light water reactors through 1981, then no more; advanced converter transition follows same pattern as breeder transition, i.e., 10 percent in 1975, 20 percent in 1976, etc.; additional assumption given in table 6–8.

Table 6–11. Uranium requirements for power for two variations of date of breeder introduction (in thousands of U$_3$O$_4$ short tons)

Year	Breeder introduction in 1980		Breeder introduction in 1990	
	Annual requirements	Cumulative requirements from 1 January 1966	Annual requirements	Cumulative requirements from 1 January 1966
1975	11 (10)	40 (39)	11 (10)	40 (39)
1980	24 (17)	124 (111)	18 (15)	103 (96)
1985	45 (36)	287 (231)	33 (21)	221 (182)
1990	64 (59)	551 (460)	75 (37)	495 (319)
1995	65 (60)	874 (761)	102 (73)	914 (573)
2000	57 (53)	1,186 (1,052)	117 (97)	1,474 (1,007)
2005	40 (36)	1,442 (1,289)	101 (84)	2,030 (1,473)

Note: Requirements with advanced converters in growth pattern are given in parentheses.

Assumptions: Reference nuclear capacity projection, breeder reactor transition follows pattern: 10 percent of capacity addition first year is breeder, 20 percent second year is breeder, etc. (following AEC in *Analysis of Advanced Converters*); a total plant factor of .8 is applied through 1980, declining linearly to .7 in 1990, and .7 thereafter; plutonium is recycled in light water reactors through 1981, then no more; advanced converter transition follows same pattern as breeder transition, i.e., 10 percent in 1975, 20 percent in 1976, etc.; additional assumption given in table 6–8.

in chapter 4, about four pounds of tails, or depleted uranium, are produced per pound of 2.5 percent enriched uranium. Therefore, quite roughly, four-fifths of the total uranium requirements given in the tables will be stockpiled in the form of depleted uranium. This stockpile is of course finite and will not meet breeder demands forever. But for well past the horizon of this analysis, the supply of depleted uranium should be sufficient.

The second assumption is that plutonium will be recycled in light water reactors and will continue until four years prior to the introduction of breeders. The reason for the ending of recycle is that the marginal product of plutonium in breeder reactors is greater than in light water reactors. Hence, breeder operators should pay more for plutonium than the value of the plutonium in light water recycle. The four-year lead time is to allow for the cooling, recovery, and fabrication of the plutonium to prepare it for breeder inventory.

The reserves given in table 6–9 represent the AEC estimates of the tons of U_3O_8 likely to be supplied at each price level. We must emphasize that these estimates are as of 1966. Since our predictions of uranium requirements cover the period 1966–2005, it seems rather anomalous to compare a dynamic demand with a static supply, but unfortunately there is no alternative. We are assuming no shifts in the supply function, due either to technical change or to new discoveries. Indeed, this may be a very misleading assumption. Two AEC officials have stated:

> We feel confident that vigorous search will uncover substantial new uranium reserves which can be mined as cheaply, or nearly as cheaply, as those now being exploited. . . . While no one can predict with any certainty the size of uranium ore reserves which remain undiscovered, it does not seem unreasonable to assume that discoveries in the next twenty years will be at least equal to those of the last twenty years, and they may be much larger.[46]

A quite significant amount of uranium has already been accumulated by the AEC. The question which naturally arises is: What fraction of these reserves will be available for civilian nuclear power?

> The figure of 275,000 tons of U_3O_8 for past deliveries to the AEC (through 1/1/65) would, at face value, appear to be an extremely important U.S. uranium resource. We assume, however, that nearly all of this material has been processed for plutonium and U-235 production and thus exists today as a stockpile of isotopically depleted uranium, presumably in the form of UF_6 "tails" from the AEC's isotope separation

46. Rafford L. Faulkner and William H. McVey, "Fuel Resources and Availability for Civilian Nuclear Power, 1964–2000," paper given at the Third United Nations International Conference on the Peaceful Uses of Atomic Energy, Geneva, August 1964, p. 9.

plants. . . . Some of the U-235 and plutonium now reserved for defense purposes could conceivably become available for blending with depleted material to provide fuel for civilian power reactors. . . . In the main, however, the depleted uranium stockpile cannot properly be classed as a fuel resource for the power industry until the advent of breeder reactors.[47]

Of the U_3O_8 to be delivered to the AEC under the stretchout program, a certain portion is to be made a government U_3O_8 stockpile. Following the assumption made in *Outlook for Uranium,* we have added 30,000 tons to the reserves given in table 6-9 to represent this portion.

Another potential source of uranium, extraction from the sea, was announced in 1964 by a British scientist at the Third United Nations International Conference on Peaceful Uses of Atomic Energy. Dr. Robert Spence, head of the British Atomic Energy Research Center, mentioned "a recovery cost of about $20 a pound" and that "the Florida current, sweeping out of the Gulf of Mexico, carried some two million tons of uranium past Key West every year."[48] This source may prove economic in the long run, but it will certainly not be a significant factor in the next few decades.

We shall return now to a closer examination of tables 6-9, 6-10, and 6-11. Our basic aim is to draw whatever information we can from the tables about future price, but we are also interested in the relative pressures on price which certain key parameters may exert. One interesting question is the comparative effect on price of growth patterns with and without advanced converters. The effect on price of varying dates of breeder introduction is also relevant.

All five cases show that cumulative requirements in 1980, with and without advanced converters, are less than reasonably assured reserves at a price of $8 per pound of U_3O_8. That is to say, without any additions to currently known reserves, each variation of uranium demand intersects the reserves schedule at a price of $8 or less. Advanced converters make very little difference in the 1980 cumulative requirements: in the standard case (table 6-9), cumulative requirements with advanced converters are only 7 percent smaller than requirements without them. In all cases, annual requirements in 1980 are less than the current total nominal mill capacity.

In the standard case, current reserves at $10 and under appear sufficient for requirements through 1990 with advanced converters and through 1985 without them. Cumulative requirements with advanced converters in 1990 are 28 percent less than requirements without them. Annual operating re-

47. *Outlook for Uranium,* p. 16.
48. *New York Times,* 8 September 1964. Also, R. Spence et al., "Extraction of Uranium from Sea Water," *Nature,* 203 (12 September 1964): 1110–1115.

quirements in 1990 will take a total mill capacity of from 39,000 to 51,000 tons (compared to a total nominal mill capacity of 22,500 tons in 1961). An interesting point is that 1990 cumulative requirements are higher for the case in which breeders were introduced in 1980 (table 6–11) than for the standard case (breeders introduced in 1985). By 1995, however, the reverse condition holds, and by 2005 the 1980 breeder case has requirements 10–17 percent less than the standard case (10 percent less with advanced converters and 17 percent less without them). There are two reasons for the lag in the impact of breeders on requirements: (*a*) plutonium recycle is discontinued in light water reactor shortly before breeder introduction, thereby raising light water makeup requirements, and (*b*) a fraction of the early breeders are uranium-235 fueled with sizable inventory requirements.

The estimates of uranium reserves by price category can only be viewed as a supply function if pure (or nearly so) competition is expected to prevail in uranium. Since the supply side of the industry in 1970 will consist of about ten firms, the degree of competition to be expected is debatable. To the extent that competition is lacking, our estimates of price will be low.

We assume that the supply function remains stationary while we shift the cumulative demand functions along it. Clearly, price will rise over time, but the very important question of what happens to the supply function over time must not be neglected. New discoveries of uranium reserves or technological change in mining and milling can easily be imagined to shift the supply function. Future prices would then rise more slowly or even fall.

Any prediction of future uranium prices is subject to a large degree of uncertainty, especially so for predictions extending more than five or ten years into the future. Nevertheless, since the price of uranium significantly affects the inputs of our benefit-cost model, some judgment must be made. *Outlook for Uranium* includes a long-range price prediction made from the standpoint of the utility industry, and a long-range price prediction has also been made by Richard H. Graham of General Electric. These predictions and the ones used in this analysis are given in table 6–12.

Outlook for Uranium also reports the general view of producers, as gleaned from interviews:

> They tend not to be explicit about what would constitute a viable price level for an expanding uranium industry, but the impression was received that they have in mind a level somewhere between $7 and $9 starting around the mid-seventies and extending for an indefinite period.[49]

We have chosen a prediction (for the case without advanced converters)

49. P. 44.

Table 6–12. Uranium price prediction (in dollars per pound U_3O_8)

			This analysis	
Year	*Outlook for Uranium*	Richard Graham	without advanced converters	with advanced converters
1975	7	4.5	6	6
1980	7	4.5	6.5	6.5
1985	8	4.5	8	7.5
1990	9	4.5	9	8.5
1995	11	4.5	11	10
2000	14	4.5	14	12

Source: Outlook for Uranium, pp. 46, 49; Richard H. Graham, "Nuclear Fuel Cost Trends under Private Ownership," paper given at the American Power Conference, April 1965, p. 5.

which is higher than Graham but slightly lower than that of *Outlook for Uranium* or the uranium producers. In fact, our price prediction differs from the *Outlook for Uranium* prediction only in 1975 and 1980. The amount of the difference is purely judgmental, based upon our results reported earlier.

We have estimated the prices for the case with advanced converters in the following manner. Since the critical prices for our purposes are relative prices, we shall view the prediction for the case without advanced converters as a reference prediction. Then the price differences can be estimated

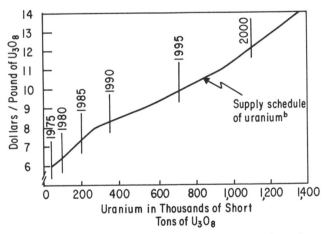

Figure 6–1. Determination of uranium prices for case with advanced converters[a]

[a] Vertical lines indicate cumulative uranium requirements for case with advanced converters on date shown.

[b] Reference price prediction versus cumulative uranium requirements for case without advanced converters.

123

by comparing relative uranium requirements for the two cases. Thus figure 6-1 shows a curve determined by reference prices and corresponding cumulative uranium requirements (from table 6-9). To obtain uranium prices for the case with advanced converters, we assume that this curve is the relevant uranium supply schedule (of course this makes the strong assumption that dynamic properties of uranium demand are unimportant). Hence, the intersection of cumulative uranium requirements (with advanced converters) for a given year with the supply schedule determines the price for that year.

In principle, for each of the cases in tables 6-9, 6-10, and 6-11, a different uranium price prediction could be made; for example, uranium prices for the case when breeders are introduced in 1985 should (possibly) differ from those for the 1990 breeder introduction case. But in our view an attempt at such precision of estimation for relatively small changes in uranium demand is impractical. The uranium prices employed in the benefit-cost analysis will therefore be assumed to be determined only by the two major cases: the case with and the case without advanced converters.

Chapter 7. Public Investment in the Development of Advanced Converters

Having completed our rather lengthy analysis of light water nuclear power cost, we can now return to the central theme of this study: an economic evaluation of the advanced converter development program. Before proceeding with the analysis of this particular government investment, it will improve our perspective to consider the rationale for public participation in this area and the alternatives in atomic power development.

Rationale for Government Participation

The prevailing ideological belief in this country is that government is justified in intervening in the economy only when the market mechanism is inefficient or ineffective. For example, if an investment yields benefits which are not in the form of identifiable and marketable goods, the private sector might not undertake projects which yield high social benefits; thus government participation is justified—indeed, necessary.

In our view, one can argue on grounds of economic efficiency that government should intervene where the price system fails, subject to the condition that social benefits must exceed social costs. Whether or not public investment in nuclear power development falls under the heading of market failure is therefore not the critical economic criterion. The ultimate economic criterion in this study is the impact on resource allocation: social benefits must be greater than social costs.

It is nevertheless of interest to examine the "case" for government intervention in nuclear power development. The testimony of Dr. Chauncey Starr, president of Atomics International, to the Joint Committee on Atomic Energy provides a good basis for discussion. In response to a question from Senator Pastore about the appropriate conditions for governmental intervention in nuclear power development, Dr. Starr stated that

> one cannot expect individual companies or individual utilities to undertake investments the payoff time of which is 20 or 30 years and the magnitude of which is so great that it represents more than the capability, in a monetary sense, of the individual corporations or companies involved.[1]

1. *Development, Growth, and State of the Atomic Energy Industry,* p. 512.

This statement illustrates two points regarding market failure. The first can be explained as follows. Large investments in highly uncertain research and development projects are generally undertaken by private firms only if the expected return is higher than for less risky projects[2] and the risk is sufficiently offset by other independent projects. By the law of large numbers, the more independent projects a firm undertakes, the less the variation of the firm's average return.

Because of the inability of firms to diversify their investments sufficiently, and because of the requirement for higher expected returns to compensate for the uncertainty, the private sector may invest in fewer research and development projects than are socially desirable. One remedy is that the government should intervene. Society, acting through government, can support a larger number of independent projects than any firm, thereby enabling society to encounter less variability in its average return than would a private firm.

The second type of market failure illustrated by Dr. Starr's statement is that the rate of interest determined in the market may be higher than the social rate of time preference. It is even argued by some that the government borrowing rate, generally conceded to be the "riskless" rate, is too high. Following this argument, the private sector may discount expected benefits from investments to lower present values than is socially desirable. This alleged divergence between the market and social rate clearly becomes quite important for projects with long payoff times, such as the development of advanced converter reactors. "This point of view can be defended as a way of compensating for market bias due to private 'myopia' or intertemporal 'selfishness'; but it raises issues beyond the scope of the [economic] efficiency criterion."[3]

A third possible reason for government participation in nuclear power research and development is the external-economy problem.

A profit-maximizing firm will undertake a research project to solve problems related to a development effort if the expected gains—for example, reduction in development costs, or improvement in the final developed product—exceed expected research costs and if total research and development cost is exceeded by the expected net value of the invention. To the extent that the results of applied research are predictable and relate only to a specific invention desired by a firm, and to the extent that the firm can collect through the market the full value of the invention to society, opportunities for private profit through ap-

2. Some might take issue with such a flat assertion of the prevalence of so-called positive risk aversion. They would point to the gambler, for example, as an example of risk preference.
3. J. Hirshleifer, "Investment Decisions under Uncertainty: Application of the State-preference Approach," *Quarterly Journal of Economics,* 80 (May 1966): 269.

plied research and the optimum quantity of a society's resources will tend to be thus directed.[4]

Thus the relevant question is whether a firm, upon successfully developing an advanced converter, would be able to capture the total social benefit attributable to that development. The answer is clearly negative. Part of the benefit would be captured by firms imitating the innovator firm, part would be captured by private utilities, and part by consumers.

A frequently voiced justification for AEC participation in advanced converter development is conservation of uranium. We dealt briefly with conservation as a proper objective of public policy in chapter 1, where it was argued that conservation, if properly conceived, coincides with the objective of economic efficiency, or optimal intertemporal allocation of resources. Admittedly, this is a rather narrow interpretation of the word; but attempting to employ the more generally accepted meaning of conservation would "invoke considerations to which economics has not much to contribute."[5]

> The conservation movement, to be sure, as a socio-political phenomenon, quickly broadened out to embrace much more, including public health, conservation of the morals of youth, elimination of child labor, preservation of natural beauty, "the elimination of waste in education and war, the conservation of manhood, and the conservation of the Anglo-Saxon race." As President Taft said, with some justice: there are a great many people in favor of conservation, no matter what it means.[6]

There seem then to be legitimate economic grounds for public participation in nuclear power development. We reject, for our analysis, the arguments for conservation of uranium in the usual meaning of that phrase and for the need to correct for market bias due to private myopia in time preference, but we accept the argument that government should consider undertaking large and risky investments which are rejected by the private sector. We also agree that external economies associated with advanced converter development might be such as to make the investment desirable for society but undesirable for a firm. Thus the next step is to evaluate the efficiency of the advanced converter investment in terms of benefits versus costs. First, however, we shall consider some of the other alternatives available to government in the development of atomic power.

4. Richard R. Nelson, "The Simple Economics of Basic Scientific Research," *Journal of Political Economy,* 67 (June 1959): 340.

5. Edward S. Mason, "The Political Economy of Resource Use," in Henry Jarrett, ed., *Perspectives on Conservation* (Baltimore: Johns Hopkins Press, 1958), p. 182.

6. Ibid., p. 155.

Alternatives in Nuclear Power Development

Some alternative development patterns available to the AEC are: (*a*) to develop advanced converters for commercial operation in the mid-1970s, and breeders for operation in the mid-1980s (preferred alternative of AEC); (*b*) to develop breeders only, for the mid-1980s; (*c*) to accelerate breeder development in order to have economic breeders before the 1980s; and (*d*) to end AEC participation in reactor development. Figure 7–1 depicts these alternatives in the form of a decision tree diagram.

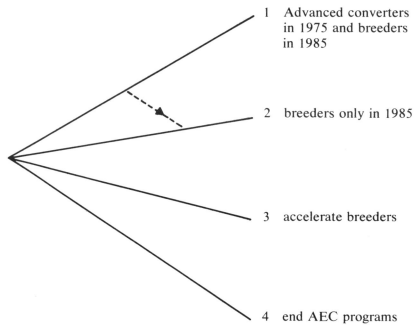

1   Advanced converters in 1975 and breeders in 1985

2   breeders only in 1985

3   accelerate breeders

4   end AEC programs

Figure 7–1. Decision tree diagram of alternatives in nuclear power development

These four alternatives are by no means exhaustive; one can contemplate many variations. It may also be contended that our decision tree should include alternatives in other energy industries, e.g., developing fuel cells or oil production from shale. Representative Chet Holifield, chairman of the Joint Committee on Atomic Energy, has suggested the following alternatives:

We have several alternatives. We could, of course, "put all our eggs in one basket" and plunge ahead into the development of the breeder reactor while leaving it to private industry to meet growing nuclear power demands. The danger is obvious. If there should be an extended delay due to technical difficulties in developing the breeder technology, we could find that all of our known domestic sources of economic uranium will be exhausted before the breeder objective is achieved.

Alternatively we could perhaps take the radical step of discouraging the growth of nuclear power until we have successfully developed the breeder. The peril here is that much of the scientific and engineering advancements that come from the design and construction and operation of nuclear plants will be lost.

Finally, we can continue the proven formula of cooperation between industry and Government and use it to take the next sequential step — the development of advanced converters. We can markedly increase the available nuclear fuel supply while profiting from the technical improvements that come from designing and constructing new plants. And this entire program can be carried out as we move toward the ultimate objective of the breeder reactor.[7]

We should note a rather important additional alternative which is illustrated by the dotted line in figure 7–1. The dotted line represents the possibility that further information gained in advanced converter development might indicate that ending advanced converter development prematurely would be desirable. That is to say, if the AEC chooses to develop advanced converters, this choice is not irrevocable. Any time that the most recent knowledge points to advanced converters as being uneconomic, further expenditure on their development could and should be stopped. Although this is a real and important alternative, we shall not attempt to take it into account in our analysis.[8]

To make a proper investment analysis, we should compare the benefits and costs of each of the alternatives. Unfortunately, because of the limited scope of this study, we can only compare the first two alternatives. As we stated in chapter 1, we shall assume that advanced converter development will have no significant effect upon breeder development; consequently, the advanced converter investment will not be credited with any benefits from the breeder program. The benefits and costs of breeder development can be omitted since they would be identical for either alternative.

In the next section we shall first discuss some general considerations pertaining to benefit-cost analysis and then turn to the measurement of benefits and costs of the advanced converter program. We shall also deal with the

7. Chet Holifield, "A Year of Decision: The Step beyond Competitive Nuclear Power," speech at Atomic Industrial Forum, American Nuclear Society Conference in San Francisco, 30 November 1964, pp. 4–5.

8. Once the development of advanced converters is thoroughly under way, vested interests may make a swift termination of the program, even though desirable, quite unlikely. That is to say, we should expect to see all prototype construction, once begun, carried through to completion.

129

difficult problems of treatment of uncertainty and selection of the appropriate discount rate. The final section will be devoted to an interpretation of the results of the analysis, and to conclusions.

Benefit-Cost Analysis

Briefly, benefit-cost analysis is a practical way of evaluating all the relevant social benefits and costs of a project in an attempt to assess its desirability. The literature on this subject in recent years is impressive.[9] Understanding the theory of benefit-cost analysis "involves drawing on a variety of traditional sections of economic study – welfare economics, public finance, resource economics – and trying to weld these components into a coherent whole."[10]

We seek to apply benefit-cost analysis to social investment in the development of advanced converter reactors. Kenneth J. Arrow has excellently described the essence of the problem of social investment:

> Investment is the allocation of current resources, which have alternative productive uses, to an activity whose benefits will accrue over the future. The cost of an investment is the benefit that could have been derived by using the resources in some other activity. An investment, then, is justified if the benefits anticipated are greater than the costs. This, of course, is an optimality condition for any productive activity.
>
> The central problem in the evaluation of investments in general is commensuration over time. Benefits accrue at different times from each other and from the costs. To add up the benefits, we must establish rates of exchange between benefits at different times, weights to be assigned to the benefits before adding them together; the same procedure must be followed for costs.[11]

Arrow goes on to explain that there are two reasons for not assigning equal weights to benefits in different time periods. The first reason is time preference: generally, present benefits are preferred to equal future benefits. The second reason is the opportunity cost of capital. "If there exists an alternative investment capable of yielding a benefit of, say, 1.10 units of benefit a year hence for a present cost of 1 unit, then the given investment, to be justified, must be capable of yielding at least as much."[12]

In our analysis, we shall rely on the opportunity-cost criterion (discount

9. For example, see the bibliography of ninety articles, books, etc., given by A. R. Prest and R. Turvey in "Cost-Benefit Analysis: A Survey," *Economic Journal*, 75 (December 1965): 683–735.

10. Ibid., p. 683.

11. "Criteria for Social Investment," *Water Resources Research*, 1 (First Quarter 1965), pp. 1–2.

12. Ibid., p. 2.

benefits and costs by the opportunity cost of capital) insofar as this is a necessary condition for the efficient allocation of resources over time. We shall assume that "time preference has already been allowed to operate in the determination of the over-all volume of investment [in the economy] and, therefore, indirectly in the determination of the rate of return on alternative investments."[13]

It will be fruitful to define the present value of future benefits as the current amount of resources which, if expended in the alternative investment, could yield the same benefits. Thus the present value of benefits, PVB, is

$$PVB = \sum_{t=1}^{T} B_t/(1 + r)^t \qquad (7\text{-}1)$$

where B_t = benefit in year t
   r = rate of return on alternative investment
   T = last year of analysis.

Clearly, if PVB exceeds the planned current expenditure of resources, or cost, the investment is justified. Selection of the alternative investment would entail a higher cost of current resources for the same benefits.

All benefit-cost analyses include a number of simplifying assumptions; real world data are never adequate for the requirements of theory. We shall use the criterion of economic efficiency, even though this ignores any unfavorable effects on income distribution. The standard assumption is that the gainers can compensate the losers and leave at least one gainer better off after the investment. We also ignore the problem of budgetary constraints. That is to say, if the AEC has limited funds, it must suboptimize; its relevant alternative rate of return may be higher than the appropriate alternative rate for the economy as a whole. In other words, the budget may force the AEC to forego projects with higher returns than are actually being undertaken elsewhere in the economy. Although it is admittedly unrealistic, we justify our assumption on the grounds that the budget itself should be determined by considerations of productivity. An exogenously determined budget "implies that the funds are available and will be spent regardless of the projects under consideration."[14]

Implicit in the discussion of alternative or opportunity cost is the assumption that full employment of resources exists. If in the absence of the investment a resource would not be used, then the appropriate opportunity price for that resource may be zero.

A number of other assumptions are required before benefits can actually

13. Ibid., p. 3.
14. J. Hirshleifer, J. DeHaven, and J. Milliman, *Water Supply, Economics, Technology, and Policy* (Chicago: University of Chicago Press, 1960), p. 149.

be calculated. The next part will explain how benefits are to be measured, and the following part will explain our choice for the proper alternative rate of return or discount rate. We shall also explain the related question of the treatment of uncertainty in that part.

Measurement of benefits. The benefits expected from the advanced converter program are taken to be the cost saving in the production of electricity. Thus we seek to measure the reduction in the future cost of producing electricity in the United States attributable to the advanced converter plants. Our procedure for measuring this cost saving will draw heavily upon the methods used in chapter 6 for calculating uranium requirements with and without advanced converters. In that chapter we computed the time path of advanced converter capacity, based upon a number of assumptions as to the rate of growth of total nuclear capacity, the rate of transition from light water to advanced converter plants, and the date of breeder introduction. Assuming future production costs, we can therefore calculate the total cost of producing electricity by advanced converters over, say, the next fifty years. Similarly, assuming that advanced converters are not developed and that the relevant capacity will be supplied by light water plants, we can compute the total alternative cost of producing electricity. The difference between these costs of producing electricity defines the time stream of benefits.

In measuring benefits, we are assuming that the costs for each type of plant reasonably reflect opportunity costs of resources used. For example, if the costs of light water plants were largely determined by inputs priced in monopolistic markets, whereas the prices for inputs in advanced converter plants were set in competitive markets, the number of benefits would be misleading (the resource cost could, in fact, be less for light water than for advanced converter plants). However, the plants have many common inputs — e.g., uranium, turbine-generators, and steel — which consequently reflect the same ratio of marginal cost to price. We thus conclude that the distortion, if any, will not be great.

Note that nothing has been said about the sign of the benefits. In fact, it is possible to have negative benefits if light water production costs are lower than advanced converter production costs.[15] Also, as is true for our analysis, it is possible to have negative benefits in the early years, changing to positive benefits in later years (depending of course upon the relative yearly cost estimates of the two types of plants). Although these negative benefits in early years could be added to the costs of advanced converter development,

15. Utility investment in the higher-cost advanced converter plants would be limited, and then only by reason of poor cost forecasts or for experimental purposes.

we prefer to subtract them from positive benefits accruing in later years. Thus our estimates of benefits should properly be termed estimates of net benefits.

Given the relevant yearly electrical capacity for the two types of plants (from chapter 6), we should examine the benefit calculation procedure in somewhat more detail. To illustrate, we shall calculate benefits for a typical year, say year t. There are two types of cost which must be treated: capital cost and fuel cost.[16]

Capital cost is the simpler of the two to treat. Total light water capital cost in t is equal to the product of the t capital cost in dollars per kilowatt and the relevant capacity addition, in kilowatts, in t. Similarly, using the t advanced converter unit capital cost, we can calculate total advanced converter capital cost in t. The difference represents our measure of benefits due to capital cost saving in t. Algebraically,

$$B_c^t = C_{lw}^t A^t - C_{ac}^t A^t \qquad (7\text{--}2)$$

where B_c^t = benefits due to capital cost saving in year t

C_{lw}^t = unit capital cost of light water plants in year t

C_{ac}^t = unit capital cost of advanced converter plants in year t

A^t = relevant capacity addition in year t.

The benefits due to fuel cost saving in t equals the product of the total number of kilowatt-hours produced by the cumulative relevant capacity in t and the difference in unit fuel costs of the two types of plants in t. Since in year t the cumulative capacity consists of plants of different vintages, it would be incorrect to assume that every plant produced the same output (all plants are assumed to be of 1,000-megawatt capacity). We have therefore assigned plant factors (utilization rates) to plants according to age; a plant of vintage t in t is assigned a plant factor of 85 percent, while a plant of vintage $t-25$ in t is assigned a plant factor of 70 percent.[17]

It is also true that in year t, plants of different vintages will have slightly different fuel costs. To a large degree, however, older plants in a given year

16. Operation and maintenance and nuclear insurance costs are omitted because these costs are assumed to be the same for light water and advanced converter plants, thereby canceling in the calculation of benefits.

17. We have chosen the following plant factors by age of plant:

Years	Plant factor (percentage)
1–5	85
6–10	85
11–15	85
16–20	80
21–25	70
26–30	50
over 30	0

will be able to incorporate fuel-cost-reducing innovations practiced by the newer plants. For a given year we shall then assign a single equilibrium fuel cost to all plants. Expressing the calculation algebraically,

$$B_f^t = \sum_{v=1}^{t} A^v \, \pi_v^t \, (F_{lw}^t - F_{ac}^t) \qquad (7\text{--}3)$$

where B_f^t = benefits due to fuel cost saving in year t
       A^v = relevant capacity addition in year v
       π_v^t = plant factor in year t for plant of vintage v
       F_{lw}^t = unit fuel cost of light water plant in year t
       F_{ac}^t = unit fuel cost of advanced converter plants in year t.

Thus the total of B_c^t in equation 7–2 and B_f^t in equation 7–3 is a measure of benefits due to the advanced converter program in year t.

Actually, the benefits defined above might be termed total "direct" benefits in order to distinguish them from another type of benefits. These other benefits, which we shall call "indirect" benefits, are relatively small in magnitude, but we should not ignore them. The indirect benefits are the savings in production costs which light water nuclear plants, coexisting with advanced converter plants, would enjoy because of the lower price of uranium brought about by a nuclear power complex with advanced converters. For example, in chapter 6, we predicted that the price of uranium in 1985 would be $8 per pound without advanced converters and $7.50 with them. The product of the kilowatt-hours generated in nonadvanced converter nuclear plants in 1985 and the saving per kilowatt-hour resulting from the lower uranium price would define the indirect benefits in that year.

Annual indirect benefits clearly will vary depending upon the uranium price differential and the number of relevant kilowatt-hours. The uranium price differential, in turn, will vary depending upon the rate of growth of nuclear capacity and the date of breeder introduction. The relevant kilowatt-hours will also be affected by these factors, but since the amount of benefits from this source is small relative to direct benefits, we shall make only one estimate of the amount and use it for all cases. Assuming that advanced converters *are* introduced successfully into the system, we shall take the following values to be indirect benefits: a present value of $25 million at a discount rate of 10 percent, and $7 million at 15 percent.[18]

18. The calculation assumes that nonadvanced converter nuclear capacity is 62,000 megawatts in 1985 (for assumptions, see table 6–9). Also, the relevant time path of kilowatt-hours is generated by that capacity operating 7,000 hours per year from 1985 to 2016 (last year of analysis). Table 4–9 gives the cost saving to be 0.0375 mills per kilowatt-hour for a $0.50 lower uranium price. Thus the annual indirect benefit is $16 million. And the present value of a stream of annual savings of $16 million from 1985 to 2016 is $25 million at a discount rate of 10 percent and $7 million at 15 percent.

In the next few sections we shall be concerned with the more important direct benefits only; for the sake of brevity we shall omit the adjective "direct." The amounts of indirect benefits will not be required again until we reach table 7–4 and figure 7 1. There we shall combine direct and indirect benefits and compare the total with program costs.

At this point we turn to perhaps the most difficult task of the analysis: the selection of specific numbers to serve as our best estimate of the future unit costs of light water and advanced converter nuclear plants. Since advanced converters are assumed to be introduced into power systems in 1975, one set of cost estimates is needed for that date, and we have chosen to make another set of cost estimates for 1985. The estimates for the intervening period lie on a curve of the form, cost $= \alpha e^{\beta t}$ (where t is time and α and β are constants determined by the 1975 and 1985 estimates).

We also make the assumption that costs in 1986, and thereafter, remain at the 1985 level. It can of course be argued that rising uranium prices will increase costs in the post-1985 period; on the contrary, one can speculate on factors making for cost decreases, e.g., technological change. On balance, we prefer the assumption of constancy of costs.

Our best estimates for these two dates are given in table 7–1. The table also gives "low" and "high" estimates; these estimates are simply 10 percent less than and 10 percent greater than our best estimates. (It could be argued that the range of uncertainty is greater for advanced converters than for light water plants, but we have elected to ignore this point.)

Light water plant costs. The assumptions underlying the light water cost estimates are given in table 7–1. Lengthy analyses, made in earlier chapters, support most of the assumptions, but in some cases the only justification for the assumption is that, in our judgment, it is reasonable. For example, we feel that it is reasonable to assume a downward shift of 5 percent in the fabrication and reprocessing cost functions over the 1975–1985 interval.[19] As will be discussed later, we shall assume that technological change of the same relative magnitude affects the fabrication and reprocessing cost functions of firms serving advanced converter plants.

Advanced converter plant costs. Cost estimates for the high-temperature,

19. This shift in the cost function is, of course, not equivalent to a movement along the function. Cost reductions resulting from economies of scale in fabrication and reprocessing are accounted for by the assumption of total nuclear power capacity. For example, we have assumed that economies of scale corresponding to a nuclear industry of 16,000 megawatts are available in 1975, and similarly, corresponding to a nuclear industry of 32,000 megawatts in 1985. The divergence between the capacities just mentioned and the AEC prediction of nuclear capacity for 1975 and 1985 is intentional; the purpose is to correct for the rather ideal assumptions made in construction of the cost functions (see chapter 5).

Table 7-1. Cost estimates for benefit-cost analysis

	1,000-megawatt light water plants		1,000-megawatt advanced converter plants (high temperature, gas-cooled)	
	Capital (dollars per kilowatt)	Fuel (mills per kilowatt-hour)	Capital (dollars per kilowatt)	Fuel (mills per kilowatt-hour)
1975				
Low	108	1.22	112.5	1.40
Best(or medium)	120	1.35	125	1.55
High	132	1.49	137.5	1.71
1985				
Low	99	0.99	94.5	0.90
Best(or medium)	110	1.10	105	1.00
High	121	1.21	115.5	1.10

Note: Low estimates are 90 percent of best estimates; high estimates are 110 percent of best estimates.

Best estimate assumptions: (a) *Light water:* Natural uranium, $6 per pound of U_3O_8 in 1975 and $8 in 1985; separative work cost, $28 per kilogram in 1975 and $25 in 1985; plutonium credit, $9 per gram in 1975 and $13 in 1985; shipping cost, $5 per kilogram both dates; plant factor, 80 percent both dates; thermal efficiency, 31.1 percent in 1975 and 33.0 percent in 1985; interest on working capital, 10 percent both dates. Multipliers of (or factors — see chapter 5) the fabrication and reprocessing cost functions and the exposure function are 1.0, 1.0, and 1.0, respectively, in 1975, and 0.95, 0.95, 1.05 in 1985, capital cost — see chapter 3. (b) *Advanced converter:* Natural uranium, $6 per pound of U_3O_8 in 1975 and $7.50 in 1985; separative work cost, same as for light water; in general the thirty-year average total fuel cost of 1.35 mills per kilowatt-hour given in the Rosenthal report (p. 201) was adjusted to represent equilibrium cycle fuel costs in 1975 and 1985 (see text); similarly, the Rosenthal report unit capital cost estimate of $118 per kilowatt (p. 84) was adjusted to the 1975 and 1985 dates (see text).

gas-cooled (HTGR) nuclear plant, our representative advanced converter, must be based on much less evidence than is available for the light water plant. In fact, these estimates must be based primarily upon data provided by the manufacturing firm which is promoting the HTGR. Fortunately, Oak Ridge National Laboratory (ORNL) has studied the data and made appropriate revisions for comparability with the light water plant. These revised estimates are given in the Rosenthal report.[20]

The Rosenthal report arrives at the figure of 1.35 mills per kilowatt-hour as its best estimate of the HTGR fuel cycle cost.[21] Relevant assumptions not suitable for our analysis are: (a) the 1.35 mills is a 30-year average fuel cost, (b) natural uranium is $8 per pound of U_3O_8, and (c) 15,000 megawatts of HTGR electrical capacity are in operation. Therefore, in order to obtain reasonable figures to use for fuel costs in 1975 and 1985, we must make some adjustments.

Since we are interested in the equilibrium fuel cycle cost for each year, the 30-year average is too low for early years and too high for later years. For one HTGR case, the Rosenthal report shows that the equilibrium cycle cost is 0.34 mills less than the 30-year average cost.[22] "The difference between the 30-year costs and the equilibrium costs is identifiable with the less favorable conditions existing when the reactor is started up with U-235 feed rather than U-233 and with the necessity for doing more fuel fabrication and processing at the beginning."[23] Since all HTGR's in 1975 will be new, they will have a disadvantage in cost because of the requirement for initial fueling with U-235; it is therefore reasonable to take the 1975 fuel cycle cost to be greater than the average. We shall increase the 1.35 mills figure to 1.55 mills for our first adjustment.

Two other adjustments are needed to arrive at a fuel cost for 1975: (a) a correction for the lower price of U_3O_8 in 1975 ($6 per pound) compared to the $8 per pound assumed in the Rosenthal report, and (b) a correction for the fact that there will obviously not be 15,000 megawatts of HTGR capacity in existence in 1975 (since, by assumption, the fabrication and reprocessing costs depend upon industry throughput of fuel, these costs are much lower with 15,000 megawatts than with essentially zero capacity).

The magnitude of the first correction can be estimated from a table in the Rosenthal report which shows the effect on fuel cost of changes in the price of natural uranium,[24] hence we should have a decrement to fuel cost of 0.075

20. M. W. Rosenthal et al., *A Comparative Evaluation of Advanced Converters*, Research and Development Report ORNL-3686, January 1965. Referred to hereafter as the Rosenthal or ORNL report.
21. Ibid., p. 201.
22. Ibid., p. 197.
23. Ibid.
24. Ibid., p. 203.

mills. But based upon our study of the economies of scale in fabrication and reprocessing for light water fuel, we judge that the second correction should be of roughly the same magnitude and of opposite sign. We shall therefore use 1.55 mills per kilowatt-hour as our best estimate of the HTGR fuel cycle cost in 1975.

We must now adjust the 1.35-mills figure to obtain an estimate of HTGR fuel cost for 1985. The first adjustment is similar to the one applied in our 1975 estimate, though opposite in sign. That is to say, the equilibrium cycle cost is lower than the average cost: we shall assume a subtractive correction of 0.20 mills.

Two other adjustments also have the effect of reducing the 1.35-mills average cost: (a) economies of scale in fabrication and reprocessing resulting from a larger amount of HTGR installed capacity and (b) technological change which is assumed to shift the cost functions downward. We shall assume each adjustment to reduce average fuel cost by 0.05 mills. Hence, at this point, the adjusted 1985 estimate is 1.05 mills.

We have predicted earlier that the relevant natural uranium price in 1985 will be $7.50 per pound (compared to the price of $8 per pound assumed for the 1.35-mills estimate) and that the separative work cost will be $25 per kilogram (compared to $30 per kilogram). The lower uranium price should reduce the 1985 estimate by 0.02 mills, and we shall assume that the lower separative work cost will increase the correction to 0.05 mills. Our best estimate of the HTGR fuel cycle cost in 1985 is therefore 1.00 mills per kilowatt-hour.

We turn now to estimating HTGR capital costs in 1975 and 1985. Here, the Rosenthal report is again helpful. On the assumption that the HTGR plant "was one of a number of the same type to be built and that the equipment and system for the plant had been fully developed,"[25] the Rosenthal report gives an estimate of $118 per kilowatt for a 1,000-megawatt plant.[26] Another assumption was that the "technology to be used in the reactor plants was generally restricted to that which would be available for a smaller, prototype reactor to be built for startup in 1970."[27]

Clearly, $118 per kilowatt is too low for 1975, when the first plants will be built, and too high for 1985, when more advanced technology and production "know-how" are available. One arbitrary adjustment might be to select $125 per kilowatt in 1975 and $110 per kilowatt in 1985, thereby making the ORNL estimate a rough average.

The Rosenthal report estimate for a light water plant, under the same

25. Ibid., pp. 8–9.
26. Ibid., p. 84.
27. Ibid., p. 3.

assumptions applicable to the HTGR, is $133 per kilowatt.[28] Our estimates for a light water plant in 1975 and in 1985 are $120 and $110 per kilowatt, respectively. We feel that our lower estimates can be largely explained by experience in manufacturing and technology which was assumed to be at a lower level (the same as for advanced converters) in the Rosenthal report. Nevertheless, under these equivalent conditions, the ORNL did assign a lower cost to the HTGR than to the light water plant. Hence, partially to reflect this, we shall use $105 per kilowatt as the capital cost estimate for the HTGR plant in 1985.

Discount rate and uncertainty. The problems of the selection of a social discount rate and the treatment of uncertainty are inseparable (by uncertainty, or riskiness, we mean that the future stream of benefits cannot be known with certainty). Kenneth J. Arrow describes this interrelation and poses the basic problem of this section:

> The implications for the rate of discount to be applied to benefits from risky social investment are less clear. According to one view, the rate to be applied is that which obtains in the private sector for investments of equal riskiness. Another position is that the government is necessarily in a better position to bear risks than any private investor. In fact, since it is involved with so many risky ventures, the law of large numbers ensures an aggregate certainty. It is therefore argued that the rate of discount should be the pure rate . . . (usually taken to be the rate on government bonds of long maturity).[29]

Because benefits will not begin until 1975 or after, the selection of the discount rate is of particular importance in our analysis. The expression for present value of benefits, equation 7–1, makes clear that for benefits distant in time the discount rate will have a large impact. Since the private sector rate for an equally risky project would be on the order of 15–20 percent and above, while the riskless rate would be near 5 percent, we must be especially careful in choosing the proper discount rate concept for our analysis.

We have two problems. First, we must determine the proper concept: comparable private sector rate or pure rate. Second, we must determine the proper number given the concept. Our solution to the second problem will be to use a range of rates near the proper order of magnitude; we shall therefore devote most of our attention to the evaluation of the concepts. Unfortunately, we cannot do justice to the evaluation of concepts here, since prominent economic theorists continue to take opposing stands, and

28. Ibid., p. 84.
29. Arrow, p. 7.

the literature is large. Some discussions propose much more sophisticated methods for selecting the opportunity costs of public investment than we can pursue here,[30] so we shall limit our discussion to the choice between the two basic concepts listed above.

In our view, the essence of the problem is revealed by answering the question of whether risk is or is not a social cost. As Professor Samuelson has pointed out, "many risks are unavoidable to the private investor and corporation which simply do not exist for WE, Inc. [Society]. The 1923 German inflation wiped out every *rentier;* it left the real economy and taxing power virtually intact."[31] We feel that the answer to the question is a matter of degree. Risk is a more significant factor to private individuals and firms, but it is never insignificant to society as a whole. Although one might argue that government should rank its potential investments primarily by expected returns, the government should never disregard uncertainty.

Following the argument that risk is not a significant social cost leads to the criterion that government should pursue a project if the expected return exceeds the pure rate of interest, but as Hirshleifer has shown, the criterion reached in the argument above only follows in a "second-best" sense: "It would clearly be most efficient for government to borrow in order to subsidize the higher-expected-yield private investments . . . rather than for the purpose of undertaking lower-yield public investment."[32] Hirshleifer's point is, of course, applicable under the assumptions that the uncertainty of expected returns is important to the private sector and that it induces the private sector to forego some projects with high expected returns — higher than the pure rate of interest.

Our position is that it would be inefficient to discount a public project at the pure rate of interest, thereby displacing private projects with higher expected returns. Although we conclude that the appropriate alternative rate of return to use in discount benefits is not the pure rate, we must now select the proper private sector rate. It is generally accepted that there is a structure of rates: higher rates are associated with riskier enterprises. Thus the market insists upon higher expected returns for more risky research and development projects than for more certain private utility projects.

We shall assume that, from the social viewpoint, if two projects have equal expected returns but unequal variances, the lower variance project

30. For example, see the discussion by Stephen A. Marglin beginning on page 198 of A. Maass et al., *Design of Water Resource Systems: New Techniques for Relating Economic Objectives, Engineering Analysis, and Governmental Planning* (Cambridge, Mass.: Harvard University Press, 1962). See also John Krutilla and Otto Eckstein, *Multiple-Purpose River Development: Studies in Applied Economic Analysis* (Baltimore: Johns Hopkins Press, 1958), pp. 78–130.

31. P. A. Samuelson, discussion in *American Economic Review,* 54 (May 1964): 95.

32. Hirshleifer, p. 220.

is preferable.[33] We should therefore select for our discount rate that rate required by the market for investments of an equal degree of riskiness.

Based upon 1959 data, Hirshleifer, DeHaven, and Milliman have recommended 10 percent for the evaluation of water resource projects.[34] Their rate calculation was based on the composite cost of money (with a 1.0 debt-equity ratio), plus taxes (the relevant rate is *before* taxes), to private utilities.

> It must be emphasized that the 10 percent figure is not the pure interest rate but rather an estimate of the implicit marginal opportunity rate in the private sphere including the allowance for risk insisted on by the capital market, the difference between 10 percent and the pure rate of just above 4 percent representing mainly the market evaluation of the risks encountered in private utility investments considering the interaction with equity financing requirements and the tax effect thereof.[35]

Following the procedure used by Hirshleifer et al., but substituting 1965 data, we calculate a current rate of slightly less than 10 percent.[36] Since investment in advanced converter development is certainly riskier than ordinary utility investment, we shall take 10 percent to be the lower limit of our range of rates.

The difficulty in determining that rate which the market would require to finance the advanced converter project is obvious. Hence, we can only select a rate as an upper limit and investigate the effect upon project desirability of the limiting rates. As an upper limit, we shall select 15 percent. One study, based on estimates of the overall rate of return from investment in the private sector, has recommended that figure.[37] Although the concept is similar to that used by Hirshleifer et al. (an estimate of the productivity of alternative uses of capital in the private sector), they criticize the study for two reasons: (*a*) the rate of 15 percent is an average rate, while it is the marginal rate (somewhat lower) which is relevant, and (*b*) being an average rate, the figure of 15 percent does not allow for the differing degrees of riskiness of investments in the various sectors.[38]

Although he approaches the estimation of the social rate of return to capital in an entirely different manner, Robert M. Solow has estimated the

33. The variance is a measure of dispersion, or uncertainty, of the subjective probability distribution of project returns.

34. Hirshleifer et al., p. 146.

35. Ibid.

36. Hirshleifer et al. used 4.7 percent debt and 5.7 percent stock earnings yield. We used 4.6 percent and 5.1 percent, respectively, taken from U.S. Department of Commerce, *Survey of Current Business,* 46 (March 1966): S-20. Note also that 10 percent is the reference rate we used in chapter 5 for working capital.

37. J. A. Stockfisch, *The Interest Cost of Holding Military Inventory* (Los Angeles: Planning Research Corporation, 1960), p. 11.

38. Hirshleifer et al., p. 147.

rate in the United States to be in "the 15–20 percent range, and perhaps even higher if we neglect housing and think mainly of business investment."[39] A rate of 15 percent is therefore not unreasonable for the upper limit, and may be too low. We shall also report results for rates of 20 and 25 percent.

Measurement of uncertainty. Our argument for the use of a high discount rate has been based to a large extent upon the great uncertainty associated with the advanced converter program. It is therefore incumbent upon us to develop the problem of uncertainty more explicitly.[40]

Perhaps the best expository procedure is to explain how we determine the expected value of benefits. This is the figure, after all, to which we should apply our discount rate. First, we select those major parameters which affect the benefits. Second, we select those values of parameters which we regard as most likely to occur; in fact, we assign a subjective probability distribution to each parameter. Third, using these probability distributions, we calculate the probability distribution of outcomes, or "states of nature." By the formulas described earlier, we then compute the present value of benefits corresponding to each possible state. The mathematical expectation of this distribution of benefits is the desired expected value of benefits. (The mathematical expectation is defined by the formula $X = \sum_i p_i x_i$, where x_i is the value of the ith possible outcome and p^i is the probability of its occurrence. For a large number of trials, the average mean outcome would be X.) And the standard deviation of this distribution provides us with a measure of uncertainty. (The standard deviation is the square root of the variance. The variance is defined by $V = \sum_i p_i (x_i - X)^2$. For a normal distribution and a large number of trials, one can expect about 68 percent of the outcomes to lie within one standard deviation of the mean. By the Bienaymé-Chebychev theorem, which applies to all distributions, not more than 25 percent of the probability can lie outside plus or minus two standard deviations from the mean.)[41]

We shall select four major parameters: (a) the rate of growth of total nuclear capacity, (b) the date of breeder introduction, (c) the unit cost of advanced converter electric energy, and (d) the unit cost of light water electric

39. *Capital Theory and the Rate of Return* (Amsterdam: North-Holland Publishing, 1963), p. 96. Professor Solow's method was to estimate the parameters of an aggregate production function model of the United States by econometric techniques.

40. For an excellent survey of current methods used in treating uncertainty, see the discussion by Robert Dorfman beginning on page 129 of the Maass et al. volume.

41. Harold Freeman, *Introduction to Statistical Inference* (Reading, Mass.: Addison-Wesley 1963), p. 31.

energy. For simplicity, we shall assume that each parameter can take on only one of three discrete values. Specifically, the first two parameters can take on those values which we used in the analysis in chapter 6. The rate of growth of total nuclear capacity will be equal either to the reference (AEC) rate or to plus or minus 10 percent of that rate (see table 6–7 in chapter 6). The date of breeder introduction will be 1980, 1985, or 1990. The three values for each of the last two parameters, the unit costs of advanced converter and light water plants, are given in table 7–1 in this chapter, i.e., the low, medium, and high estimates.

Figure 7–2, generally termed a tree diagram, permits us to show graphically all of the possible outcomes of our assumed model. To preserve neatness in the diagram we have omitted showing repetitious branches. At each of the nodules denoted by letters, branches identical to the ones extending from the center nodule, E, should be imagined. The number of possible outcomes or states (the extreme points on the right, denoted by numerals) is large, even for this simple model; there are, in fact, eighty-one states.

To illustrate the applicability of subjective probabilities to this model, we

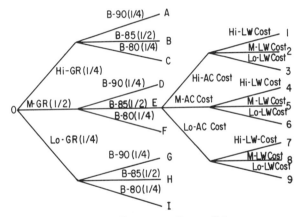

Figure 7–2. Tree diagram of possible outcomes of advanced converter program

Symbols: Hi, M, and *Lo* prefixes are high, medium, and low estimates; *GR* is growth rate of total nuclear capacity; *B-90, B-85,* and *B-80* are breeders introduced in 1990, 1985, and 1980; *AC Cost* is unit energy cost of advanced converter plants; *LW Cost* is unit energy cost of light water plants.

Note: Branches identical to those extending from nodule *E* should be imagined to extend similarly from nodules *A, B, C, D, F, G, H,* and *I.* The fractions given in parentheses are subjective probabilities for the occurrence of that particular branch.

143

shall consider one specific outcome — E-5. Beginning at the left, at nodule O, we observe three branches: high growth rate of total nuclear capacity (Hi-GR), medium growth rate (M-GR), and low growth rate (Lo-GR). Since we feel that the medium growth rate is most likely to occur, we shall arbitrarily assign it a probability of 0.50. The other two possibilities are assigned probabilities of 0.25 each. We now face the next stage — three branches represent the possible dates of breeder introduction: breeders introduced in 1990 (B-90), breeders introduced in 1985 (B-85), and breeders introduced in 1980 (B-80). We shall subjectively assign probabilities of 0.25, 0.50, and 0.25 to B-90, B-85, and B-80, respectively. Therefore, the probability of state E occurring (medium growth rate of nuclear capacity and breeders introduced in 1985) is the product of the probabilities, 0.50 and 0.50, or 0.25.

In a similar manner, probabilities can be assigned to the branches of the last two stages. Probabilities can be assigned to the occurrence of high, medium, and low advanced converter costs (the third stage) and also to the occurrence of high, medium, and low light water costs (the fourth stage). If the probability of both advanced converter and light water costs taking on their medium estimates is 0.50 each, then the probability of benefits associated with state E-5 is the product of the probabilities of the four branches defining that outcome, or 0.50 to the fourth power, 0.0625.

The probabilities we have assigned to the first two stages are shown in figure 7–2, but the probabilities we have assigned to the last two stages require further explanation. These probabilities are shown in figure 7–3, and it is apparent that we have assigned different probabilities to branches extending from the different lettered nodules. The reason is that the probabilities are conditional upon the state defined by those nodules. For example, nodule A is the state in which the rate of growth of nuclear capacity is high and breeders are introduced late, in 1990. Compared with nodule I, in which the growth rate is low and breeders are introduced early, uranium price should be higher. We therefore feel that it is reasonable to assign greater probabilities to the occurrence of high costs for the nodule A state than for the nodule I state.

It is perhaps unnecessary to labor the point that all probabilities are simply reflections of our own research beliefs. Although we think that they are reasonable, it is completely legitimate to argue that certain of the numbers should be revised. In fact, the tables which follow will, we hope, facilitate the computation of the expected value of benefits for different values of the probabilities.

Table 7–2 gives the results of the calculations of benefits for each of the possible states. (As explained earlier, these are *direct* benefits only.) Each outcome can be identified by a letter and numeral corresponding to the tree

144

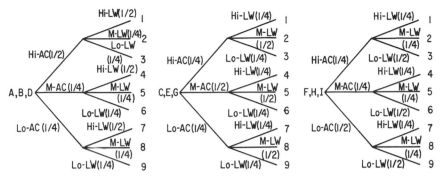

Figure 7-3. Cost branches of tree diagram of advanced converter program

Symbols: Hi, M, and Lo prefixes are high, medium, and low estimates of unit electric energy costs of advanced converter (AC) and light water (LW) plants.

Note: Three identical sets of cost branches are presented above in order to show that different subjective probabilities are assigned depending on which nodule (of figure 7-2) the branches extend from—e.g., the set on the left extends from nodules A, B, and D of figure 7-2. The probabilities for each branch are those fractions in parentheses.

diagram of figure 7-2. Our earlier example of state E-5 defines benefits which are shown in row E-5 of table 7-2. The second column of the table gives the probability of the benefits. Thus the probability of benefits for state E-5 is 0.0625.

As will be noted, benefits are reported in terms of present value for five discount rates: 5, 10, 15, 20, and 25 precent. Although we concluded earlier that 10 percent and 15 percent are the limits of the appropriate discount rate, calculations at the other three rates are also included.

For convenience, the expected value and standard deviation of benefits for each discount rate are reported at the bottom of the table. The expected values are weighted averages of the present value of benefits corresponding to each of the eighty-one states. The weights, of course, are the probabilities that the particular outcomes will occur. The standard deviations are more complex, being the square roots of another set of weighted averages. In this case the weighted averages are obtained by summing the products of the appropriate probabilities and the square of the difference between benefits and the expected value of benefits.

One further explanation is required before turning to the cost side of the analysis. Benefits have been calculated in accordance with the expression and estimates described previously, but no mention was made of the appropriate time horizon for benefit calculation. The length of the horizon is clearly important for low discount rates. Since we have chosen a lower limit of 10 percent to our discount rate (a relatively high rate), we have selected

145

Table 7-2. Present values of advanced converter program benefits (in millions of dollars)

State	Probability of state	Discount rate				
		5 percent	10 percent	15 percent	20 percent	25 percent
A-1	.0156	2,802	753	235	82	30
A-2	.0078	0	0	0	0	0
A-3	.0078	0	0	0	0	0
A-4	.0078	6,587	1,940	674	265	115
A-5	.0039	2,548	684	214	74	28
A-6	.0039	0	0	0	0	0
A-7	.0078	10,372	3,126	1,112	448	199
A-8	.0039	6,333	1,871	652	258	112
A-9	.0039	2,293	616	192	67	25
B-1	.0313	1,579	459	153	56	22
B-2	.0156	0	0	0	0	0
B-3	.0156	0	0	0	0	0
B-4	.0156	3,859	1,259	478	202	93
B-5	.0078	1,435	417	139	51	20
B-6	.0078	0	0	0	0	0
B-7	.0156	6,139	2,060	803	348	164
B-8	.0078	3,715	1,218	464	197	91
B-9	.0078	1,292	376	125	46	18
C-1	.0039	668	202	69	25	9
C-2	.0078	0	0	0	0	0
C-3	.0039	0	0	0	0	0
C-4	.0078	1,846	672	282	130	64
C-5	.0156	607	184	63	23	9
C-6	.0078	0	0	0	0	0
C-7	.0039	3,024	1,142	494	235	119
C-8	.0078	1,785	659	275	128	63
C-9	.0039	546	166	56	21	8

D-1	.0313	2,016	545	171	59	22
D-2	.0156	0	0	0	0	0
D-3	.0156	0	0	0	0	0
D-4	.0156	4,774	1,422	500	199	87
D-5	.0078	1,833	495	155	54	20
D-6	.0078	0	0	0	0	0
D-7	.0156	7,531	2,300	830	339	152
D-8	.0078	4,590	1,373	485	194	85
D-9	.0078	1,650	446	140	48	18
E-1	.0156	1,171	341	113	41	16
E-2	.0313	0	0	0	0	0
E-3	.0156	0	0	0	0	0
E-4	.0313	2,889	950	363	155	72
E-5	.0625	1,064	310	103	37	14
E-6	.0313	0	0	0	0	0
E-7	.0156	4,607	1,560	614	269	128
E-8	.0313	2,782	919	353	151	70
E-9	.0156	958	279	93	34	13
F-1	.0078	514	155	52	19	7
F-2	.0078	0	0	0	0	0
F-3	.0156	0	0	0	0	0
F-4	.0078	1,439	527	222	103	51
F-5	.0078	467	141	48	17	6
F-6	.0156	0	0	0	0	0
F-7	.0156	2,364	898	391	187	95
F-8	.0156	1,392	513	217	101	51
F-9	.0313	420	127	43	15	6
G-1	.0039	1,440	391	123	43	16
G-2	.0078	0	0	0	0	0
G-3	.0039	0	0	0	0	0

Table 7-2. Present values of advanced converter program benefits (in millions of dollars) (continued)

State	Probability of state	Discount rate				
		5 percent	10 percent	15 percent	20 percent	25 percent
G-4	.0078	3,438	1,037	369	149	66
G-5	.0156	1,309	355	112	39	14
G-6	.0078	0	0	0	0	0
G-7	.0039	5,435	1,683	615	255	116
G-8	.0078	3,307	1,001	358	145	64
G-9	.0039	1,178	320	100	35	13
H-1	.0078	861	251	83	30	11
H-2	.0078	0	0	0	0	0
H-3	.0156	0	0	0	0	0
H-4	.0078	2,147	712	275	118	55
H-5	.0078	783	228	76	27	10
H-6	.0156	0	0	0	0	0
H-7	.0156	3,433	1,174	466	206	99
H-8	.0156	2,069	689	267	115	54
H-9	.0313	705	205	68	25	9
I-1	.0039	392	118	39	14	5
I-2	.0039	0	0	0	0	0
I-3	.0078	0	0	0	0	0
I-4	.0039	1,113	409	173	81	40
I-5	.0039	357	107	36	13	4
I-6	.0078	0	0	0	0	0
I-7	.0078	1,834	701	307	147	76
I-8	.0078	1,077	399	169	79	40
I-9	.0156	321	96	32	11	4
Total expected value		1,564	490	180	74	33
Standard deviation		1,880	591	221	93	44

Note: Value of parameters which define each state are given in figure 7–2.

fifty years as the length of the analysis. Benefits accruing in later years have negligible present values. In this connection it is of interest to examine the time profile of the present value of benefits; table 7–3 provides such a time profile for state E-5 – the state in which all four parameters take on their medium, or our best, estimates.

Table 7–3. Present values of benefits, by year, for state E-5

	Discount rate	
Year	10 percent	15 percent
1975	−1.8	−1.2
1976	−2.9	−1.9
1977	−3.8	−2.3
1978	−3.7	−2.2
1979	−2.7	−1.5
1980	−0.4	−0.2
1981	3.1	1.6
1982	8.1	4.0
1983	14.5	6.8
1984	22.2	10.0
1985	27.2	11.7
1986	26.4	10.8
1987	25.1	9.9
1988	23.6	8.8
1989	21.7	7.8
1990	19.6	6.7
1991	17.4	5.7
1992	15.0	4.7
1993	12.6	3.8
1994	10.1	2.9
1995	9.1	2.5
1996	8.3	2.1
1997	7.5	1.8
1998	6.7	1.6
1999	6.1	1.4
2000	5.5	1.2
2001	4.9	1.0
2002	4.4	0.8
2003	3.9	0.7
2004	3.4	0.6
2005	3.0	0.5
2006	2.7	0.4

Table 7-3. Present values of benefits, by year, for state E-5 (continued)

| Year | Discount rate | |
	10 percent	15 percent
2007	2.3	0.3
2008	2.0	0.3
2009	1.7	0.2
2010	1.4	0.2
2011	1.2	0.1
2012	0.9	0.1
2013	0.7	0.0
2014	0.5	0.0
2015	0.4	0.0
2016	0.3	0.0
Total	309.7	103.0

Note: Values of the parameters which define state E-5 are given in figure 7–2; benefits are in millions of dollars.

Costs of the advanced converter program. The cost of the advanced converter program must now be estimated. Of course, the relevant cost is the marginal or future cost; past research and development costs are "sunk" and therefore irrelevant. There are two types of costs we should consider: government (AEC) and private sector.[42] AEC costs for the entire program have been estimated to be about $300 million,[43] obviously a highly uncertain figure. For example, although the $300 million estimate was made in 1965, it already requires revision to reflect the 1966 AEC recommendation that the scheduled seed and blanket prototype project be postponed.[44] Since future developments will undoubtedly induce both increases and decreases in total AEC cost, we shall select the $300 million figure as our best estimate.

Again, we should point out that the current advanced converter program consists of three types of reactors: (*a*) high-temperature, gas-cooled (HTGR), (*b*) heavy-water, organic-cooled (HWOCR), and (*c*) seed and blanket (SBR). We have based our analysis on the costs of the HTGR, selected as a representative advanced converter. Clearly, the AEC has a number of alternatives within the advanced converter program itself. For

42. Another type of cost—the opportunity cost incurred as a result of producing uneconomic electric power—has been accounted for in the benefit calculations.

43. The estimate was made by AEC Chairman Seaborg and Commissioner Ramey and includes "the cost of the prototypes, work directly related to the prototypes, and the associated research and development work" (*AEC Authorizing Legislation Fiscal Year 1966, Part 3,* p. 1386).

44. *Nucleonics,* 24 (February 1966): 18.

example, the AEC could concentrate on the HTGR exclusively, thereby saving development costs on the HWOCR and the SBR. Of course it can be argued that this alternative would also reduce the probability of developing a successful advanced converter. The question is whether or not the increased cost of a three-reactor program is worth the increased probability of success. Certainly the evaluation of the technical and economic potential of each of these reactors requires continuing analysis. Unfortunately, the amount of the increase in probability of success attributable to a three- rather than one-reactor program is somewhat beyond the technical competence of this analyst (we shall, however, make an illustrative calculation of this later).

Another problem related to the AEC development cost is that we have no way of relating changes in costs to changes in benefits. In principle, we should like to have a function relating these two. Then the optimal investment would be determined by increasing development costs until marginal cost equals marginal benefit. Since we have no such function, we must measure benefits and costs as if they were independent.

Advanced converter development costs of the private sector, not covered by sales or by the AEC, are also relevant. For example, Gulf General Atomic is committed to the development of the HTGR and has a contract with the Public Service Company of Colorado to construct a 330-megawatt HTGR prototype plant.[45] AEC will pay about $47 million, and the utility will pay about $46 million;[46] other costs of Gulf General Atomic would be relevant. Also, any excess in the cost of producing power over that of an alternative plant is relevant (we only account for uneconomic power in 1975 and after in our benefit calculations—the Colorado HTGR plant is scheduled for operation in 1971). The president of the utility has stated, however, that from the utility's viewpoint the power will not be uneconomic: "Our estimated cost at the buss would be about 4.5 mills. I might say roughly comparable with the alternatives which we have."[47]

Private sector development costs are even more difficult to estimate than are AEC costs; nevertheless, they should not be ignored. The tendency for cost estimates to be lower than actual costs should also be considered; for example, the cost estimates for the first five original reactors in the AEC's experimental pilot-plant program increased "from 36 percent to 89 percent above their original estimated costs."[48] Since there is no objective

45. *AEC Authorizing Legislation, Part 3, Fiscal Year 1966*, p. 1829.
46. Ibid., p. 1830.
47. Ibid., p. 1552.
48. Richard Tybout, "Atomic Power and Energy Resource Planning," *Federal Expenditure Policy for Economic Growth and Stability* (Washington: Government Printing Office, 1957), p. 775.

way to arrive at a figure which accounts for these factors, we shall arbitrarily increase the $300 million estimate to $400 million. To allow for the uncertainty, we shall assume a range of total development cost estimates: $300 million, $400 million, and $500 million.

The time distribution of these costs is also important. Since the development phase should cover about nine years (1966 to 1974), we shall divide the total cost into nine equal annual costs. For our medium, or best, cost estimate ($400 million), the annual cost will then be $44.4 million.[49] The present values of the cost streams have been calculated for five discount rates (see table 7–4).

Interpretation of Results and Conclusion

Before attempting to assess the results, we should like to quote from a study on the social returns of atomic power by Edward F. Renshaw, who has excellently expressed the philosophy underlying our own work in this field.

> It is not without hesitation that one attempts an analysis which even at its inception may be out of date. Research, by its nature, is concerned with the isolation of relationships and parameters that are unknown; it is difficult to imagine a situation in which resources are committed that entails greater uncertainty. Uncertainty as to the magnitude of the costs and returns associated with the development of new techniques, however, is not an excuse for ignoring information and expectations which do exist or can be made readily available for guiding decision making; we still want to be as confident as possible that resources invested in research are put to their highest alternative use.[50]

The results of our benefit-cost analysis are presented in table 7–4 and figure 7–4. Figure 7–4 leads us to the conclusion that the break-even point is about 13 percent. Thus if the alternative rate of return is below that point, the advanced converter program is desirable, and vice versa. Another way of expressing the same thing is that benefits exceed costs at 10 percent and benefits are less than costs at 15 percent. Since 10–15 percent is the range of rates we consider to be proper, our results unfortunately do not provide us with a decisive argument either for or against the program. The program, under the assumptions of our model, is neither strongly desirable nor strongly undesirable.

49. AEC estimated spending for advanced converters in fiscal year 1967 is $45.8 million, including $19.3 million on the HTGR, $14 million on the HWOCR, and $12.5 million on the SBR. See *Nucleonics*, 24 (March 1966): 22.
50. Renshaw, p. 222.

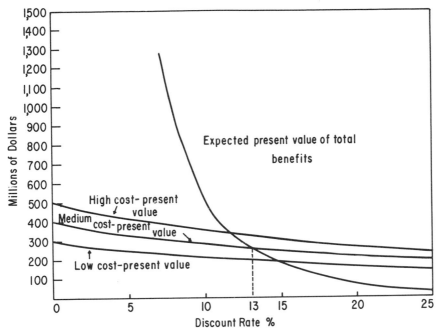

Figure 7–4. Expected value of benefits versus cost, for advanced converter program

We must certainly not neglect the critical nature of some of our assumptions. Perhaps the most important is the use of cost estimates for the advanced converters which are based primarily upon data provided by the sponsoring manufacturer. Clearly the manufacturer has good reason to be optimistic in its cost predictions.

We should also point out the importance of only very small differentials in unit power costs. For example, the cost assumptions for table 7–3 are such that the total cost saving per kilowatt-hour in 1994 is 0.1 mill. Despite the tiny unit differential, the number of kilowatt-hours produced in that year is so large (1.46×10^{12}) that the product is also large (even at a discount rate of 10 percent the present value of 1994 savings is $10 million).

Although we have assumed probability distributions for the important parameters, the means of the distributions are our best estimates and consequently have a large effect on the expected value of benefits. Consider the date of breeder introduction. Recent announcements by General Electric, Westinghouse, and Atomics International that they expect to start construction of large breeder prototypes in the near future indicates that

153

Table 7-4. Present values of benefits and costs of advanced converter program (in millions of dollars)

	Discount rate				
	5 percent	10 percent	15 percent	20 percent	25 percent
Expected value of direct benefits[a]	1,564	490	180	74	33
Expected value of indirect benefits[b]	68	17	5	2	1
Total benefits	1,632	507	185	76	34
Low cost	249	211	183	161	144
Medium cost	331	281	244	215	192
High cost	414	352	305	269	240
Benefits less medium cost	1,301	226	−59	−139	−158

[a] See table 7-2.
[b] See pp. 134–135. Expected value is obtained by multiplying indirect benefits by the probability that the advanced converter program is successful (the sum of the state probabilities in table 7-2 associated with direct benefits greater than zero). For example, at 10 percent, the product of $25 million and 0.69 is $17 million. Note that the probability is 0.31 that indirect benefits will be zero.
Assumptions: Low cost, medium cost, and high cost represent total cost estimates of $300 million, $400 million, and $500 million, respectively. Costs are assumed to be incurred in equal amounts in each year of the period from 1966 to 1974.

154

breeders might be economic earlier than 1985 (our best estimate).[51] For the state defined by medium estimates for all parameters except breeder introduction date, and a breeder date of 1980, the program is uneconomic for all discount rates within our range of rates. This state, *F*-5, has total benefits of $166 million at 10 percent, while costs are $281 million. At 15 percent, benefits are only $55 million, while costs are $244 million.

On the other hand, the AEC has recently raised its prediction of the growth rate of nuclear capacity. If we should decide that the latest AEC prediction is better than the earlier prediction (which we have adopted), our calculated expected value of benefits would be too low.[52] The effect of a higher growth rate can be shown by examining the benefits corresponding to state *B*-5 (high nuclear growth rate – 84,000 megawatts in 1980 – and best estimates for other parameters). Total benefits at 10 percent are $442 million compared to costs of $281 million, but the project is still uneconomic at 15 percent, with benefits of $146 million versus costs of $244 million.

The heart of this discussion is that uncertainty is extremely important. Although our effort to present a probability distribution of benefits makes uncertainty somewhat more explicit, the only adjustment for uncertainty has been in the selection of "risky" discount rates. Whether the ratio of the standard deviation to the expected value of benefits is similar to private sector ventures requiring expected returns of 10–15 percent is an open question.

Perhaps our best single summarizing remark is that the advanced converter program is apparently a marginal project *if* the advanced converter estimates of unit costs are good. Were the time and resources available, it would be interesting to conduct a poll of informed people in the industry concerning their subjective probabilities of the major parameters – especially of advanced converter unit costs.

On the basis of the foregoing analysis, we are reluctant to recommend a cancelation of the entire advanced converter program, but on economic grounds we do feel that there is strong justification for a rapid paring down of the program to one reactor type.[53] That is to say, the benefits hardly

51. *Nucleonics*, 24 (April 1966): 22–23. Also, the British announcement of an estimated cost of 3.4 mills per kilowatt-hour for a 1973-construction-start breeder is an additional indication that the breeder introduction date of 1985 might be too late (*Nucleonics*, 24 [July 1966]: 25).

52. Our best estimate is 74,000 megawatts in 1980; the 1966 AEC estimate has a mean of 95,000 megawatts in 1980 (*Nucleonics*, 24 [July 1966]: 23). As of 1969 the AEC estimate of 1980 capacity stood at 150,000 megawatts!

53. Three years have elapsed since this recommendation was made in 1966. Therefore, a few remarks about the status of the advanced converter program in 1969 seem appropriate here. As of 1969, the best estimate of the date of commercial breeder introduction continues to be 1985. The AEC has greatly increased its estimate of the growth rate of nuclear capacity (see n. 52), but since 1967 new orders for nuclear capacity have fallen sharply. Higher costs

justify a complete development program (including large prototype demonstration) for all three types of reactors. The attractiveness of the investment would be greatly enhanced if costs could be cut by two-thirds while expected benefits remain substantially the same.

As discussed earlier, it can be argued that the probability of developing at least one successful advanced converter would be reduced if the AEC eliminated two of the three reactors from the program. Although we do not feel competent to estimate the probability reduction, or even to select the single best reactor concept, we can illustrate the proper type of calculation with an example. Assume that the probability distributions for advanced converter unit power costs are changed in the following way to reflect the elimination of two of the three reactor concepts: the fraction $\frac{1}{8}$ is added to the probabilities of the high-cost estimates, and the fraction $\frac{1}{8}$ is subtracted from the probabilities of the low-cost estimates. For example, the probabilities of the branches extending from nodules A, B, and D (see figure 7–3) are changed to show probabilities of $\frac{5}{8}$, $\frac{1}{4}$, and $\frac{1}{8}$ for high, medium, and low advanced converter costs, respectively. Of course, the development cost of the program is assumed to be reduced by $\frac{2}{3}$. The results of the "one-reactor" program as compared with the results of the original, or "three-reactor" program are shown in table 7–5. Clearly, under the assumptions of our example, the "one-reactor" program is the more desirable investment.

Since the administration of the development program requires sequential decision-making rather than one-time decision-making, we strongly recommend that continuous evaluation within the benefit-cost framework be undertaken. Even better, since benefit-cost analysis is necessarily a partial analysis, we urge that a more general programming approach to public investment in energy research and development be undertaken. Elaborate cost-reducing development programs in nuclear energy are foolish if nuclear energy is only economic because of government restrictions in other energy

---

and increased public concern with nuclear safety and environmental effects have reduced the attractiveness of nuclear plants to electric utilities. For example, in 1966 nuclear plants accounted for 53 percent of total new orders for electric capacity, while the corresponding figure for the first nine months of 1969 was only 13 percent. Consequently, although we may have understated the benefits of the advanced converter program by our use of a growth rate that was too low, the AEC 1969 estimate would appear to be too high. Finally, although the *absolute* costs of nuclear plants have risen substantially since 1966, we have little basis for predicting the effect on our results since it is the *relative* costs of light water and advanced converter reactors that enter the benefits calculation.

The advanced converter program, as of 1969, is centered on the SBR and the HTGR. The HWOCR was abandoned in 1968. Research spending for fiscal year 1970 was estimated to be $15.4 million for the SBR and $2 million for the HTGR. In addition, the AEC is continuing to support the construction of the 330-megawatt HTGR plant in Colorado, scheduled for operation in 1972 U.S. Atomic Energy Commission, *The Nuclear Industry 1969*, December 1969, p. 163.

Table 7-5. The three-reactor program versus the one-reactor program (amounts in millions of dollars)

Discount rate	Three-reactor program		One-reactor program	
	Benefits	Cost	Benefits	Cost
10 percent	$507	$281	$397	$94
15 percent	185	244	143	81

industries, e.g., oil import quotas and coal-carrying railroad transport rates.

One final comment would appear to be appropriate. Our analysis has been concerned exclusively with the advanced converter program in the United States. Thus our results apply solely to this country and imply nothing about the desirability of similar programs in other countries. Clearly, the incentive for a program in other countries will depend upon the relative costs of the first-phase nuclear plants and advanced converter plants, the amount of expected nuclear capacity, the status of breeder development, and the expected program cost.

List of Works Cited

Adelman, M. A. "Efficiency of Resource Use in Crude Petroleum." *Southern Economic Journal* 31 (October 1964):101–122.

———. *The Supply and Price of Natural Gas.* Supplement to the *Journal of Industrial Economics.* Oxford: Basil Blackwell, 1962.

Arrow, Kenneth J. "Criteria for Social Investment." *Water Resources Research* 1 (First Quarter 1965):1–8.

Arthur D. Little, Inc. *Competition in the Nuclear Power Supply Industry.* December 1968.

———. *The Outlook for Central-Station Nuclear Power in the United States.* September 1964.

Atomic Industrial Forum. "Financing Privately Owned Nuclear Fuel Inventories." Report of the Ad Hoc Committee on Financing Nuclear Fuels. February 1963.

———. *A Study of the Possible Effects of Private Ownership of Nuclear Fuels and Toll Enrichment on Uranium Markets.* April 1964.

Baldwin, C. J., et al. "Economic Aspects of System Expansion with Nuclear Units." *Power Apparatus and Systems.* February 1963.

Benedict, Manson, and Pigford, Thomas H. *Nuclear Chemical Engineering.* New York: McGraw-Hill, 1957.

Benham, Isabel H. "Can the Railroad and the Coal Industry Meet the Challenge of Lower Atomic Power Costs?" Address before Cleveland Society of Security Analysts, 7 October 1964.

Chittenden, W. A. "Nuclear or Fossil: How Do You Choose?" *Electrical World,* 2 May 1966, 72–74.

Davis, Harold L. "How Big Will Power Plants Get?" *Nucleonics* 21 (June 1963): 60–63.

Davis, W. Kenneth, and Roddis, Louis H., Jr. "A Projection of Nuclear Power Costs." In National Industrial Conference Board report, *Fifth Annual Conference: Atomic Energy in Industry.* 1957.

Dragoumis, Paul, et al. "Estimating Nuclear Fuel-Cycle Costs." *Nucleonics* 24 (January 1966):40–45.

Edison Electric Institute. *Plutonium Survey, 1964*. Prepared by the EEI Committee on Nuclear Fuels. New York, June 1965.

————. *Statistical Yearbook of the Electric Utility Industry for 1964*. New York, September 1965.

————. *Survey of Initial Fuel Costs of Large U.S. Nuclear Power Stations*. New York, December 1958.

Eschbach, E. A. "Plutonium Value Analysis." In *Proceedings of the Third United Nations International Conference on the Peaceful Uses of Atomic Energy*. Vol. 11. New York, 1965.

————. *A Survey of the Economics of Plutonium as a Fuel in Thermal Reactors,* AEC Research and Development Report HW-75338. 1962.

————. "Utilization of Plutonium in Fast and Thermal Reactors." 1963.

————, and Goldsmith, S. "Using Plutonium in Thermal Reactors." *Nucleonics* 21 (January 1963):48–52.

————, and Kanninen, M. F. *Uranium Price Schedules and Bred Fuel Value*. AEC Research and Development Report HW-72219. December 1964.

Evans, R. K. "Nuclear Power Reactors." *Power,* March 1965, pp. 167–191.

Faulkner, Rafford L., and McVey, William H. "Fuel Resources and Availability for Civilian Nuclear Power, 1964–2000." Paper given at the Third United Nations International Conference on the Peaceful Uses of Atomic Energy, Geneva, August 1964.

Federal Power Commission. *National Power Survey, 1964, Parts I and II*.

Freeman, Harold. *Introduction to Statistical Inference*. Reading, Mass.: Addison-Wesley, 1963.

Fuller, John. *The Gentlemen Conspirators*. New York: Grove Press, 1962.

Geller, L., et al. "Analyzing Power Costs for Nuclear Plants." *Nucleonics* 22 (July 1964):64–72.

Glasstone, Samuel, and Sesonske, Alexander. *Nuclear Reactor Engineering*. Princeton: Van Nostrand, 1963.

Graham, Richard H. "Nuclear Fuel Cost Trends under Private Ownership." Paper given at the American Power Conference, April 1965.

Harms, Keith L. *Economic Considerations Bearing on Civilian Nuclear Power Development*. Supplement II to the Report of the Ad Hoc Committee on Atomic Policy of the Atomic Industrial Forum, March 1962.

Hasson, J. A. *The Economics of Nuclear Power*. London: Longmans, Green, 1965.

Herling, John. *The Great Price Conspiracy*. Washington: Robert B. Luce, 1962.

Hirshleifer, J. "Investment Decisions under Uncertainty: Application of the State-Preference Approach." *Quarterly Journal of Economics* 80 (May 1966):252–277.

160

———, DeHaven, J., and Milliman, J. *Water Supply, Economics, Technology, and Policy*. Chicago: University of Chicago Press, 1960.

Hogerton, John F. *The Atomic Energy Deskbook*. New York: Reinhold, 1963.

———, Geller, L., and Gerber, A. *The Outlook for Uranium: A Survey of the U. S. Uranium Market*. A report for the East Central Nuclear Group. New York: S. M. Stoller Associates, 1965.

Holifield, Chet. "A Year of Decision: The Step beyond Competitive Nuclear Power." Speech at Atomic Industrial Forum, American Nuclear Society Conference in San Francisco, 30 November 1964.

Hollister, Hal L., and Burington, Artha Jean. "Pricing Enriched Uranium." *Nucleonics* 16 (January 1958):54–57.

Hughes, Donald J. *On Nuclear Energy*. Cambridge, Mass.: Harvard University Press, 1957.

Jersey Central Power and Light Company. *Report on Economic Analysis for Oyster Creek Nuclear Electric Generating Station*. 17 February 1964.

Koch, L. J. "The Future of Fast Breeders." *Nucleonics* 21 (June 1963): 72–75.

Krutilla, John, and Eckstein, Otto. *Multiple-Purpose River Development: Studies in Applied Economic Analysis*. Baltimore: Johns Hopkins Press, 1958.

MacAvoy, Paul W. *Economic Strategy for Developing Nuclear Breeder Reactors*. Cambridge, Mass.: MIT Press, 1969.

McCune, Francis K. "The Impact of Government Regulation on Technological Development in Nuclear Energy." In Edward J. Bloustein, ed., *Nuclear Energy, Public Policy, and the Law*. Dobbs Ferry, N. Y.: Oceana, 1964.

Maass, A., et al. *Design of Water Resource Systems: New Techniques for Relating Economic Objectives, Engineering Analysis, and Governmental Planning*. Cambridge, Mass.: Harvard University Press, 1962.

Mason, Edward S. "The Political Economy of Resource Use." In Henry Jarrett, ed., *Perspectives on Conservation*. Baltimore: Johns Hopkins Press, 1958.

Massé, Pierre. *Optimal Investment Decisions: Rules for Action and Criteria for Choice*. Englewood Cliffs, N.J.: Prentice-Hall, 1962.

Meyers, Harold B. "The Great Uranium Glut." *Fortune*, February 1964, pp. 108–111.

Mullenbach, Philip. "Government Pricing and Civilian Reactor Technology." In Henry Jarrett, ed., *Science and Resources*. Baltimore: Johns Hopkins Press, 1959.

161

Naylor, Thomas H., and Vernon, John M. *Microeconomics and Decision Models of the Firm.* New York: Harcourt, Brace and World, 1969.
Nelson, Richard R. "The Simple Economics of Basic Scientific Research." *Journal of Political Economy* 67 (June 1959):297–306.

Prest, A. R., and Turvey, R. "Cost-Benefit Analysis: A Survey." *Economic Journal* 75 (December 1965):683–735.

Ramey, James T. "A Review of Nuclear Programs of Interest to the Oil and Gas Industry." Speech at the Texas Mid-Continent Oil and Gas Association, Fort Worth, Tex., 19 October 1965.
_____. "The Role of Planning in the Atomic Energy Program." Speech at Lynchburg, Va., 16 February 1965.
Reichle, Leonard F. C. "A Private Nuclear Power Economy." *Proceedings of the Atomic Industrial Forum, 1964* 2 (December 1964):96–122.
Renshaw, Edward F. "Atomic Power: Research Costs and Social Returns." *Land Economics* 35 (August 1959):222–231.
Roddis, Louis H., Jr. "The Atom: Catalyst for a 4-mill Kilowatt-hour." *Proceedings of the Atomic Industrial Forum, 1964* 2 (December 1964): 79–95.
Rosenthal, M. W., et al. *A Comparative Evaluation of Advanced Converters.* AEC Research and Development Report ORNL-3686. January 1965.

Solow, Robert M. *Capital Theory and the Rate of Return.* Amsterdam: North-Holland Publishing, 1963.
Spence, R., et al. "Extraction of Uranium from Sea Water." *Nature* 203 (12 September 1964):1110–1115.
Sporn, Philip. "Nuclear Power Economics: An Appraisal of the Current Technical-Economic Position of Nuclear and Conventional Generation." Speech at Morgan Guaranty Hall, New York, March 1966.
_____. "A Post–Oyster Creek Evaluation of the Current Status of Nuclear Electric Generation." *Nuclear Power Economics: Analysis and Comments, 1964.* Prepared for the U.S. Congress, Joint Committee on Atomic Energy, October 1964.
Stathakis, G. J. "Nuclear Power Drives Energy Costs Down." *Electrical World,* 5 October 1964, pp. 50–53.
Stockfisch, J. A. *The Interest Cost of Holding Military Inventory.* Los Angeles: Planning Research Corporation, 1960.
Stoker, D. J., Golan, S., and Siegel, S. "Wanted: A Balanced Nuclear Economy." *Nucleonics* 21 (June 1963):79–82.

Tape, J., Pittman, F., and Searl, M. "Future Energy Needs and the Role of Nuclear Power." Paper given at the Third United Nations International Conference on the Peaceful Uses of Atomic Energy, Geneva, August 1964.

Thomas, Morgan. "Democratic Control of Atomic Power Development." *Law and Contemporary Problems* 21 (1956):38–59.

Tybout, Richard. "Atomic Power and Energy Resource Planning." *Federal Expenditure Policy for Economic Growth and Stability*. Washington: Government Printing Office, 1957.

———. *The Reactor Supply Industry*. Columbus, Ohio: Bureau of Business Research, Ohio State University, 1960.

United Kingdom, Central Electricity Generating Board. *An Appraisal of the Technical and Economic Aspects of Dungeness B Nuclear Power Station*. 1965.

U.S. Atomic Energy Commission. *AEC Gaseous Diffusion Plant Operations*. Report ORO-658. February 1968.

———. *Analysis of Advanced Converters and Self-Sustaining Breeders*. Reprinted in *AEC Authorizing Legislation, Fiscal Year 1966, Part 3*. March 1965.

———. *Annual Report to Congress of the Atomic Energy Commission for 1965*. January 1966.

———. *Civilian Nuclear Power: A Report to the President, 1962*. Oak Ridge, Tenn.: AEC Division of Technical Information, 1962.

———. *Civilian Nuclear Power: The 1967 Supplement to the 1962 Report to the President*. February 1967.

———. *Cost-Benefit Analysis of the U.S. Breeder Reactor Program*. Report WASH-1126. 1969.

———. *The Current Status and Future Technical and Economic Potential of Light Water Resources*. Report WASH-1082. March 1968.

———. *Estimated Growth of Civilian Nuclear Power*. Report TID-4500. March 1965.

———. *Methods of Calculating U-235 Outputs and Charges by Use of Ideal Cascade Theory*. Report TID-8522. February 1960.

———. *1965 Financial Report*. Washington: Government Printing Office, 1965.

———. *The Nuclear Industry, 1969*. December 1969.

U.S. Congress, Joint Committee on Atomic Energy. *AEC Authorizing Legislation, Fiscal Year 1965, Part 1*. 88th Congress, 2nd Session. March 1964.

———. *AEC Authorizing Legislation, Fiscal Year 1966, Part 1*. 89th Congress, 1st Session. January 1965.

———. *AEC Authorizing Legislation, Fiscal Year 1966, Part 3*. 89th Congress, 1st Session. March and April 1965.

———. *Chemical Reprocessing Plant*. May 1963.

———. *Development, Growth, and State of the Atomic Energy Industry*. April 1963.

———. *Development, Growth, and State of the Atomic Energy Industry*. August 1965.

———. *Future Ownership of the AEC's Gaseous Diffusion Plants*. August 1969.

163

————. *Nuclear Power Economics: Analysis and Comments, 1964.* October 1964.

————. *Nuclear Power Economics, 1962–1967.* February 1968.

————. *Private Ownership of Special Nuclear Materials, 1964.* June 1964.

U.S. Department of Commerce. *Survey of Current Business.* Vol. 46, no. 3. March 1966.

U.S. Interdepartmental Energy Study. *Energy R & D and National Progress.* Washington: Government Printing Office, 1965.

U.S. Senate Committee on the Judiciary, Subcommittee on Antitrust and Monopoly. *Economic Concentration, Part I.* July and September 1964.

————. Hearings on Administerial Prices. *Price-Fixing and Bid-Rigging in the Electrical Manufacturing Industry, Parts 27 and 28.* April, May, and June 1961.

Vallance, John M. "Economics of the Conversion of Nuclear Energy to Electricity." *Proceedings of the American Chemical Society.* Detroit, April 1965.

————. "Fuel Cycle Economics of Uranium Fueled Thermal Reactors." Paper given at the Third United Nations International Conference on the Peaceful Uses of Atomic Energy. Geneva, May 1964.

Walton, C., and Cleveland, F. *Corporations on Trial: The Electric Cases.* Belmont, Calif.: Wadsworth, 1964.

Index

Adelman, M. A., 10n., 40n., 99n.
Advanced converter reactors, 4, 17, 116, 150
Advanced thermal reactors. *See* Advanced converter reactors
Arrow, Kenneth J., 130, 139
Arthur D. Little, Inc., 37n., 47n., 106n.
Atomic Energy Commission (AEC), 3–12, 65–67, 103–105, 150–152, 155
Atomic Industrial Forum, 82, 102
Atomics International, 153

Baldwin, C. J., 108n.
Benedict, Manson, 58, 60n.
Benefits of advanced converter program, 6, 132–135, 152–157; indirect, 134; measurement of, 132–135
Benefit-cost analysis, 11, 130–157
Benham, Isabel H., 111n.
Bienaymé-Chebychev theorem, 142
Bloustein, Edward J., 40n.
Breeder: doubling time, 87; reactors, 4, 87, 116
Burington, Artha Jean, 63n.

Capacity, nuclear, 4n., 57, 97, 106–113, 155n.
Chain reaction, 14
Chittenden, W. A., 42
Cleveland, F., 40n.
Coal, 14, 109–112
Computer simulation, 108
Conservation, 6, 9, 127
Consumption cost, 25, 51
Control rods, 17
Coolant, 16
Cost: of advanced converter plants, 135–139; of advanced converter program, 150–152; capital, 12, 29–31, 109, 133; consumption, 25, 26, 51; fabrication, 25, 26, 71–76; fuel, 12, 24–29, 48–70, 109; of light water, 12, 135; marginal, 21, 67, 73,

Cost: (*cont.*)
77; reprocessing, 25, 26, 49, 76–80; shipping, 25, 26, 49, 80; uranium, 68; working capital, 26, 49, 80–83

Davis, Harold L., 42n.
Davis, Kenneth, 75, 106n.
Decision tree, 128, 143, 145
DeHaven, J., 141
Development program: advanced converter, 5, 9, 125, 128–129, 150; breeder, 5, 10, 128–129; nuclear power, 3, 128–129
Discount rate, 130, 131, 139–142, 155
Dorfman, Robert, 142n.
Dragoumis, Paul, 28n.
Dresden-2 nuclear plant, 43–46

Eckstein, Otto, 140n.
Economies of scale, 21, 25, 42, 67, 72, 76
Edison Electric Institute, 84, 110
Efficiency: economic, 67, 125–127; fuel use, 4n., 15, 16, 18; thermal, 17, 49, 90–93, 111
Einstein, A., 14
Elasticities, fuel cost, 93, 95
Enrichment: production function, 58–65; uranium, 54–70
Eschbach, E. A., 53, 62, 85n.
Evans, R. K., 17n.
Exposure, 49, 89

Fabrication cost, 25, 49, 71–76
Faulkner, Rafford L., 120n.
Federal Power Commission, 112n.
Fertile material, 15
Fissionable material, 15
Fixed charges, 30
Freeman, Harold, 142n.
Fuel: fossil, 109; nuclear, 49
Fuel cycle, nuclear, 18, 48, 49
Fuller, John, 40n.

165